This book is for my beautiful mum and my sister, Suzy, who both helped inspire a lot of these recipes, and for my very missed dad, who inspires our lives.

AIR FRYER EXPRESS

60 delicious recipes for dinners,
snacks & school lunches

George Georgievski

plum Pan Macmillan Australia

CONTENTS

INTRODUCTION

Howdy! Thank you for picking up my book. You'll have a laugh and might just pick up some tips and tricks, too. My name is George, and I'm also known as the School Lunchbox Dad ... Google it! My first book, *Lunchbox Express*, was pretty good. Good enough for my publisher to say to me 'Hey George, we know how much you love your air fryer and how popular your recipes are ... we think it's time you created your own George-style air fryer book.' And so here we are.

For those who don't know me yet, I'm a dad from Geelong, Victoria, who loves rocking out to Pearl Jam,* writing my own music and poetry, and also having fun in the kitchen. I love creating healthy and creative meals for my daughters, Anela and Kiara, and I'm a very hands-on dad. I've been married for almost 20 years to a complete stunner named Marina.

I took over cooking and lunch-making duties for my girls a few years ago and ever since I have been looking for ways to make lunches fun, healthy, simple and quick! When I first started making school lunches, I would fire up the oven each morning just to bake a few pastries or scrolls. The girls loved the food I was making, but I had to look for a faster solution.

Then, there it was, like a shining light from the heavens ... the air fryer! It was a lot more economical, required no preheating and cooked food in half the time. I was instantly inspired when I unwrapped my first air fryer. It was so easy! Just plug in and play.

It was a revelation when I discovered how much time I could save in the mornings using the air fryer. Pizza scrolls only took 8 minutes to cook compared to 25 minutes in the oven (including preheating time). That's a 17-minute difference! I could have my breakfast and espresso, as well as make my wife a single-origin filtered coffee in the time I had saved. When you are a busy parent or carer, time is of the essence.

The air fryer also gave me the opportunity to recreate some classic dishes that would usually take hours to cook in a regular oven. For example, when I was growing up, my mum would make baklava and it would take the whole day. Now I can make it in a fraction of that time (see page 135). My wife and I both work full time, so we need to save as much time as possible. I think of air fryers as smart devices. Like smart phones, they make life easier and help us to get things done quickly.

A lot of the recipes in this book are very important to me. For example, the gevrek recipe on page 127 was my grandfather's special recipe. He was a baker (maybe that's where I get my passion for cooking?) and the recipe was sent to me from my aunties in Macedonia. I used to eat many of these dishes as a kid and they fill my soul. My mum got more satisfaction from my sister and me eating her food than anything else and that's exactly how it is for me today with my girls. I get to express my love for them in the form of a beautiful dinner or a colourful and healthy school lunchbox.

I'm so excited to share this book with you because I have worked really hard developing recipes that I know you are going to absolutely love. In the following pages you'll find my air fryer 101 to help you get the most out of your air fryer, 60 insanely good air fryer recipes, as well as 30 pages of lunchbox inspiration (because many of these air fryer recipes also work brilliantly in the school or work lunchbox).

I'm no chef, I'm just a hard-working dad with a passion for creating simple and healthy food and a mission to inspire people everywhere to make life a little more magical for their kids. With this book, I hope to make it easy for you to use your air fryer to whip up delicious, creative food for your family. Follow these recipes and you'll be a kitchen rock star with loads more spare time to spend with the ones you love!

George

*Not just Pearl Jam (although I hope I meet Eddie Vedder one day). I also love NIN, Rage Against the Machine, Nirvana, '90s hip hop and basically any music that comes out of Seattle.

THE
BASICS

AIR FRYER 101

<u>Getting started</u>

If you're reading this book, it's most likely because you've recently bought an air fryer and you're looking for recipe inspiration and tips to help get you started. Or perhaps you bought my first book, *Lunchbox Express*, and loved it so much you just had to buy this one?! Yeah, that's probably why you're here ... let's go with that.

Whatever your reason for picking up this book, there are a few things I'd love to share with you to help you get the most out of your air fryer. In the coming pages, I explain why I think the air fryer is the best thing since the toaster (I was going to say sliced bread, but we all know that the toaster is responsible for making sliced bread even tastier). I also offer some advice on choosing the right air fryer, let you in on my favourite equipment to make your life easier and offer some general tips so you can wow your friends and family with super simple and delicious recipes.

If you're brand new to air fryers, let me tell you a little more about them. Essentially they are like small benchtop convection ovens with powerful fans. They are multi-functional, in that they can bake, roast and fry. They get hotter than convection ovens, though, as they are very small and so can make food that is almost as crispy as when you deep-fry – without the need for a whole lot of oil. They also have an inbuilt basket with holes in it, which allows the air to circulate around the food for even and quick cooking.

Alright, now that you know the basics of how air fryers work, let's look at why they rock, how to choose one and my top tips for getting the most out of them.

Why air fryers rock!

- **They save time** Air fryers cook food in a fraction of the time an oven takes.

- **They save money and electricity** There's no need to heat up a big oven to cook a small dish.

- **They're multi-functional** Some models can fry, bake, grill and roast.

- **They're perfect for smaller spaces** Save bench space by getting rid of some single-function appliances.

- **They're healthy** You can cook food to crispy perfection without the need for lots of oil.

- **They're versatile** You can use your air fryer to cook everything from sweet potato chips and lasagne to pizza scrolls, pavlova and so much more!

- **They're easy to use** There's usually no preheating required and absolutely anyone can use them – they will make you feel more confident in the kitchen.

- **They're safe** Air fryers stop working when the lid is opened so there is a reduced risk of burns compared to when deep-frying or using the oven.

- **They're easy to maintain** Air fryers are simple to clean, especially if you line the base with baking paper before putting food in. I much prefer pulling out the tray from the air fryer and washing it in the sink rather than bending down to scrub my oven! Most air fryers claim to be dishwasher safe, but to keep your machine in tip-top condition, hand washing is best.

- **They help reduce waste** You can use your air fryer to make delicious creations with ingredients you would usually throw in the bin. For example, when I peel potatoes, I throw the clean peels into the air fryer for a few minutes and turn them into a crunchy snack!

- **They're great for reheating** Air fryers remove moisture from food, so are much better than microwaves for reheating things like pizza or pastries as your food will become nice and crispy instead of soggy!

Choosing an air fryer

• Do some research to find the air fryer that's right for you – look at your space, get out your measuring tape and choose one that fits your own kitchen, keeping in mind it's important to leave a little space around your air fryer on the bench.

• Try to find an air fryer that is multi-functional to get the most out of it. Look for one with a grilling and baking function as well as the air fryer function.

• Air fryers vary in wattage – usually the more money you spend, the more powerful the machine and the hotter it will get.

• Looks can be deceiving. You might feel that a small air fryer will do, but once you get going, I predict you'll want to be able to fit more food in. Most are 3 litres but get a bigger one if you have the space so that you have more options (some are big enough to cook a whole chicken!).

• Choose one that is simple to look after. Fewer parts = easier to clean!

• Finally, choose an air fryer to fit your price point. No need to get fancy. You can make delicious food in the cheap and cheerful versions, too.

Equipment to make your life easier

Ramekins, ramekins, ramekins! I often use ramekins in my air fryer, as they fit well and the food cooks a little faster than in a large baking dish. Plus, who doesn't love getting their own individual dish to eat out of?

Small baking dishes Find ones that will easily fit in your air fryer.

Regular, oven-safe dinner plates and bowls These can be used in place of baking dishes – as long as they are oven safe, you can cook food in them and serve them as they come out of the air fryer. Genius!

6-hole muffin trays Small muffin trays are a great size for most air fryers.

Soft silicone utensils These will help to avoid scratching the non-stick coating inside the air fryer.

Baking paper If you want a cleaner cooking experience, keep your pantry stocked with baking paper for lining the air fryer and baking trays.

Cookware with removable handles Look for baking dishes and other cookware with removable handles – they make it much easier to get dishes in and out of the air fryer.

Protein shaker I love using a protein shaker to make small batches of things like muffin mixture or pancake batter.

1. Don't overfill the basket.

You want the air to circulate properly and cook your food evenly so don't overfill! For fries and other food that needs to be brown all over, give the basket a shake a couple of times during cooking.

2. Be prepared.

Chop and prep everything before you turn on the air fryer. You'll be surprised how quickly food cooks in it, so getting your ingredients ready ahead of time will make for a super-speedy cooking experience.

3. Always use oven mitts!

Air fryers are HOT, so use oven mitts and silicone-coated tongs to take cooked food out. Safety first, people!

My top 5 air fryer tips

4. Use olive oil spray to coat your food evenly.

Unlike cooking in a regular oven, with an air fryer we coat the food instead of the tray. This means much less oil is used, so it's healthier and also easier to clean up.

5. Be adventurous and creative.

There are no rules and there's no harm in trying something new. Say you have some leftover tortillas after a batch of soft tacos, why not cut them into triangles and pop them in the air fryer and see what happens? (Hint: you'll end up with a crunchy, delicious snack!)

LUNCHBOX FAQs

While this book is largely focused on the air fryer, I also wanted to include some tips on packing delicious, healthy and colourful lunches. I am asked so many questions on social media and at events, so I thought I'd share my answers to some of the most common ones. I hope they help to make creating school lunches easy and fun.

'I'm nervous about putting cold meat, eggs and dairy into my child's lunchbox. How can I make sure these foods will stay at a safe temperature?'

This is one of the most common questions I'm asked and it really is super simple. Just get yourself a cooler bag and an ice pack. You can use any type of cooler bag as long as it seals properly and fits the lunchbox and an ice pack. You can find both of these in most supermarkets.

'Won't yoghurts, sauces and dips leak into my child's school bag?'

Not if you use a really good-quality bento-style lunchbox. These are designed to be air- and liquid-tight, to keep food fresh and bags clean!

'I bought a bento-style lunchbox and I'm struggling to find things to fit in the small compartments.'

Use your mad knife skills and get creative with your cutting. You can make anything fit if you really want it to (see opposite!). Also, you can make your own bite-sized versions of your kids' favourite foods – try my mini croissants on page 124 or Puff Daddy dawgs on page 46.

'How do you find the time to pack such interesting and colourful lunches every single morning?'

I know mornings can be hectic, so I give myself a head start on the day and get up an hour before my girls do to make a coffee and get myself ready. Then I'm free to make my girls' lunches while they have breakfast and get ready for school. Being organised is key to an easy morning. I really enjoy getting creative and deciding each morning what to put in their lunchboxes, but I still do some prep in advance to make life easier. I make sure that the lunchboxes are clean and dry, and that all my fruit and veggies are washed. Then it's just a quick chop and assemble and we're good to go.

'How do I create a balanced and healthy lunchbox?'

Don't get too caught up thinking you have to pack all sorts of fancy things. In each lunchbox, I make sure there is a portion of protein, some veggies, dairy, fruit and a healthy treat. Keep it simple and packet free, and you can't go wrong.

'Do you have any tips on how to get the kids excited to try new things?'

Getting the kids involved can boost enthusiasm levels. Try taking them shopping with you to choose the fresh ingredients and get them to help with preparing or assembling their own lunches – even if it's just one day a week to start with. My girls love coming up with fun names for my different lunchbox creations, too. Anything that makes the process fun can help!

'When I pack veggies in my child's lunchbox, they inevitably come home uneaten. How do I get my kids to eat their veggies?'

Both of my kids are picky in different ways, and sometimes one of the six bento box compartments will come home untouched. I call the uneaten item – which is usually a new veggie – the 'risk taker'. I'll try the risk taker again the following week and then again the week after. Getting kids used to new foods is a gradual process. The key is to keep trying!

Picky eaters are more likely to try something new if it looks cool. And if you change up the presentation they never get bored. Rainbows make my girls happy, so I put a rainbow of veggies in their lunchboxes every day. Making their lunches look appealing is a great way to encourage your kids to actually eat them!

THE
RECIPES

**Delicious pastries, scrolls, bready things
and crispy bites to pimp up the lunchbox
(I promise they won't go soggy!)**

SANDWICHES
ARE
BORING!

OOZING CHEESE AND GARLIC STICKS

Makes 8–10

When I think of cooked cheese I imagine it stretching for miles and miles! This simple and fun recipe is a definite favourite – it has texture and crunch, and is also perfect for the lunchbox.

WHAT YOU'LL NEED

1 egg

2 garlic cloves, peeled

bread crusts from 4 slices of bread

pinch of salt flakes

8–10 batons of cheddar (about 10 cm long and 2 cm thick)

LET'S DO THIS!

Beat the egg in a bowl or, if you are like me, use a protein shaker to shake the egg to create an egg wash. Line the base of your air fryer with baking paper.

Grab your garlic and bread crusts, pop them in the air fryer and cook on 200°C for 3 minutes. What we are doing here is removing the moisture from the bread and slightly toasting it.

Using a blender, blitz the toasted bread, garlic and salt until you've made your very own breadcrumbs. Well done, legend! Pop the garlicky breadcrumbs on a plate.

Now for the cheese. Dip the cheese batons in the egg wash until they're fully coated, then roll them in the breadcrumbs.

Reduce the air fryer to 180°C, add the breaded cheese sticks and cook for 8 minutes or until golden brown. If you can eat just one, you deserve a medal. Otherwise, if you're like me, you'll eat the whole lot and then need to make more for everyone else.

Try using a fancy French blue cheese or even haloumi to impress your friends. Feel free to add green stuff, such as chopped parsley or oregano, to the breadcrumb mixture. If you want to get real fancy, you can pair your chosen cheese with an appropriate wine to simply blow your friends away.

To make this recipe even easier and quicker, use store-bought breadcrumbs.

PIZZA SCROLLS FOR THE LUNCHBOX

Makes 10

I've been making these scrolls for the past few years. They're super popular with my girls and they fit really snugly in their school lunchboxes. You can't go wrong with pizza! What kid doesn't like pizza?

STUFF TO GET

2 sheets of frozen puff pastry, just thawed

3 tablespoons tomato paste

small handful of basil leaves (optional)

75 g (½ cup) grated mozzarella

OKAY, GREAT – NOW WHAT?

Using a knife or a pizza cutter, cut each pastry sheet into five even strips. Grab a teaspoon and put a dollop of tomato paste in the centre of each pastry strip. Use the back of the spoon to evenly spread the paste over the strips, but avoid getting too close to the edges. At this point you can add the basil leaves or skip them and go straight for the mozzarella. Sprinkle the mozzarella along the centre of each pastry strip, again avoiding the edges.

Now for the folding and rolling. Don't stress, it's easier than it sounds. Fold the pastry strips in half lengthways, to enclose the ingredients. Don't worry if some of the grated mozzarella falls out – it's all good as we're not on *MasterChef*. Roll up the strips until you have created ten of the best ever pizza scrolls. Line the base of your air fryer with baking paper and pop the scrolls in. Cook on 180°C for 8 minutes or until golden brown.

Allow the pizza scrolls to cool, then pack into lunchboxes or put them in an airtight container in the freezer where they will keep for up to 2 months.

EXTRA, EXTRA, READ ALL ABOUT IT!

You can make vegan pizza scrolls by using non-dairy cheese. I've made them a few times and they're pretty dang good, so for any lactose-intolerant little peeps this is a genuinely awesome lunchbox addition, after-school snack or even dinner.

POCKET ROCKETS

Makes 12

These pastries are so easy and fun to whip up that they are one of the few recipes I let my girls make themselves. We always have the ingredients in the kitchen ready to go, which means they are great for unexpected guests or when the out-laws (I mean the in-laws) show up.

Pocket rockets are an excellent addition to school lunchboxes and they also make awesome party food. The filling is super flexible, so add any ingredients you want and leave out any you don't. These ones are Italian inspired, but you could use peas, finely chopped carrot and a little curry powder to take them in an Indian direction. Or see More Things below for paella pockets!

GO GRAB THIS STUFF

1 sheet of frozen puff pastry, just thawed

3 tablespoons tomato paste

75 g (½ cup) grated mozzarella

1 egg, lightly beaten

sesame seeds, for sprinkling

WHAT'S NEXT?

Find a cookie cutter or even a wine glass (some of you are probably more familiar with the latter anyway). Now grab your puff pastry sheet and cut out twelve circles of pastry. (You can roll the leftover pastry into a ball, cover with plastic wrap and return to the freezer to use another day.)

Place a pastry circle in your palm and add 1 teaspoon of tomato paste and 1 teaspoon of mozzarella. Now all you need to do is fold the pastry over the filling and pinch the edge with your fingers or with a fork to secure. It should look like a dumpling. Repeat with the remaining pastry circles and filling.

Brush the beaten egg over the pastry pockets and sprinkle a few sesame seeds on top. Line the base of your air fryer with baking paper and pop the pockets in. Cook on 175°C for 8 minutes. They should be golden and ready to eat.

 MORE THINGS Turning these into paella pockets could be a game changer. Just add 1 tablespoon of cooked rice, a pinch of smoked paprika, a couple of chopped olives and a slice of chorizo to each pastry circle to create a genius finger-food delight.

THE DAY-AFTER TOASTIE

Makes 1

We've all had that 'day-after' moment; the times when we've celebrated a little too hard and realised that we're not that young anymore. This little recipe has helped me in the past, so it's time to share with you my saving grace. Inspired by the Cubano sandwich, it is pure bliss and a fabulous pick-me-up. I don't care what anyone else says about the perfect toastie; for me, it's all about the following ingredients. So take a photo of this list and get to the supermarket (but don't drive if you're recovering from the night before).

YOU WILL NEED

1 tablespoon butter

2 x 2 cm thick slices of crusty Vienna bread

1 tablespoon American mustard

2 slices of Swiss cheese

4 cm piece of chorizo sausage, finely sliced

2 slices of cheddar

2 slices of ham off the bone

½ teaspoon smoked paprika

2 dill pickles, finely sliced lengthways, plus extra to serve (optional)

thin plain chips, to serve

OKAY, GREAT – NOW WHAT?

Butter both sides of the bread slices and let's start stacking. Here's how it works:

Smear the mustard on one side of the bread slices, then top with one slice of Swiss cheese, half the chorizo, one slice of cheddar, one slice of ham and a dusting of smoked paprika. Take a breath and get ready to keep layering. Add one slice of Swiss cheese, the remaining chorizo, one slice of cheddar, one slice of ham and the pickle. Top with the other slice of bread and finish with a dusting of paprika.

You should now have a tower of deliciousness, so what we need to do is give it a little squash (I use a frying pan to push it down, but I guess your hands will work, too).

Line the base of your air fryer with baking paper and pop the toastie in. Cook on 180°C for 5 minutes. The cheese and oil from the chorizo should be oozing out the sides, while the top of the toastie will be lovely and golden from the butter and paprika. I mean, just take a look at the picture opposite and please don't drool on your new book.

Cut the toastie on an angle because that's how everyone does it these days, top with some extra dill pickle, if you like, and serve with a handful of chips.

GRISSINI WITH HALOUMI

Serves 4 (and makes 12 grissini)

I'm forever adding grissini to Anela's and Kiara's bento boxes for school, so I figured it was time to make my own. I tried all sorts of combinations and they all pretty much rocked, but this recipe is my favourite. Cook some haloumi in the air fryer while your grissini are cooling down and you have a match made in heaven.

GRAB THE FOLLOWING

250 g (1⅔ cups) bread flour

1 teaspoon sugar

2 teaspoons salt flakes

7 g sachet dried yeast

olive oil, for drizzling

1 egg, lightly beaten

1 teaspoon sesame seeds

250 g haloumi, thickly sliced

finely grated zest and juice of ½ lemon

½ teaspoon freshly ground black pepper

½ teaspoon dried oregano

rosemary sprigs and flowers, to serve (optional)

LET'S GET CRACKING

Using a stand mixer with the dough hook attached or a whisk and a large bowl, combine the flour, sugar, half the salt and the yeast. Add 120 ml of water and mix for about 5 minutes, until a dough forms. It should look just like bread dough, and if you haven't made bread dough it should look like pizza dough, and if you haven't made pizza dough … Okay, enough is enough. Let's continue, shall we? Drizzle a little olive oil in a large bowl and smear it around the base and side. Add the dough, cover with plastic wrap and set aside at room temperature for 1–1½ hours, until doubled in size.

Tear off a golf ball–sized piece of dough and knead it briefly, then roll it into a 12 cm log about the thickness of your little finger. Transfer to a piece of baking paper and repeat with the remaining dough to make about twelve logs.

Brush the grissini with the beaten egg and sprinkle over the remaining salt and the sesame seeds. Lift up the baking paper and grissini and pop them in your air fryer to cook on 190°C for 7 minutes, keeping an eye on them to make sure they don't burn. Remove from the air fryer and allow to cool.

While the grissini are cooling down, cook your haloumi. To do this, you can simply pop the haloumi slices straight on the baking paper that the grissini were cooked on in the air fryer, or you can place the slices in individual ramekins. Cook on 180°C for 6 minutes or until golden.

Transfer the haloumi to a serving board, top with the lemon zest and juice and drizzle with olive oil. Sprinkle over the pepper and dried oregano, as well as some rosemary if you want to make things super pretty, and serve with the grissini.

BONUS AWESOMENESS

Depending on how good your baking skills are, you can try some cool twists with the grissini, such as shaping the dough sticks into mini pretzels or even simply trimming them to perfectly fit your school lunchboxes. Genius, right?

HEAVENLY BREAD ROLLS

Makes 16

There's nothing more amazing than the smell of fresh bread first thing in the morning; however, my bread-maker seems to take ages and, if you're like me, I ain't got time for that! So I did some research and testing to find a new way to make fluffy white bread rolls in the air fryer. I think this recipe will change how you make bread.

WHAT YOU'LL NEED

280 ml warm water

7 g sachet dried yeast

1 teaspoon sugar

500 g (3⅓ cups) bread flour

1 tablespoon salt flakes

1 tablespoon olive oil

olive oil spray

1 tablespoon melted butter

sesame seeds and poppy seeds, for sprinkling (optional)

WHAT'S NEXT?

I use my protein shaker for this first part, but you can also use a large jar. Place the warm water, yeast and sugar in the shaker or jar and give it a good shake for about 1 minute. Let it sit for 10 minutes to allow the yeast to activate. Place the flour and salt in the bowl of a stand mixer with the dough hook attached and mix briefly to combine. Add the yeast mixture and olive oil and mix on low speed for 10 minutes or until you have a smooth dough.

Divide the dough into sixteen even-sized balls, then place on a large tray lined with baking paper with enough space between the dough for these bad boys to spread and rise. Cover with plastic wrap and leave at room temperature for 1 hour.

Grab as many 8 cm diameter ramekins as you can find and grease them with olive oil spray. One by one, knead your dough balls for 10 seconds, then transfer to the ramekins. You can score the tops with a single line or cross, if you like, then brush a little of the melted butter over the top (you'll thank me for this later). If you want to get fancy, sprinkle on some sesame or poppy seeds.

Transfer the ramekins to your air fryer and cook on 170°C for 10 minutes. The smell will blow your mind! Repeat with the remaining dough until you've made sixteen perfectly round bread rolls.

EXTRA, EXTRA, READ ALL ABOUT IT!

I love the glossy finish the melted butter adds to the bread rolls, but sometimes I like to mix it up. Try brushing the dough with beaten egg instead or sprinkle the rolls with a little flour after they've come out of the air fryer. You got this!

EASY PEASY CHEESY BALLS

Makes 6

These cheesy balls are a cheese lover's dream. What I love most about them is how something so simple can taste so good, and, from what my girls tell me, they're the best! I do recommend using a food processor for this recipe, but a basic one will do – no need for fancy pants here. Follow this simple recipe for a cheesy time.

GET THE FOLLOWING DELIVERED

125 g (1 cup) grated cheddar

2 tablespoons grated parmesan

250 g (1 cup) natural yoghurt, plus extra if needed

350 g (2⅓ cups) self-raising flour, plus extra if needed

1 teaspoon salt flakes

1 egg, lightly beaten

1 teaspoon sesame seeds

OKAY, GREAT – NOW WHAT?

Combine the two cheeses in a bowl and set aside.

Pop the yoghurt, self-raising flour and salt in a food processor and blitz for 30 seconds or until the mixture comes together into a dough ball. You may need to add a little more flour or yoghurt to bring the mixture together.

Once the dough is looking good, divide it into six even-sized balls. Working with one ball at a time, flatten it out into a 6 cm disc and place one-sixth of the cheese in the middle of the dough. Using your hands, fold the dough over to enclose the cheese and roll the dough into a ball again. Repeat with the remaining dough and cheese.

Dunk the cheese balls in the beaten egg and sprinkle over the sesame seeds. Line the base of your air fryer with baking paper and pop the balls in. Cook on 170°C for 10 minutes. Once cooked, you can either share them or eat them all yourself. It depends on the type of person you are, and I respect you either way.

You can sprinkle extra cheese, such as grated parmesan, on top but be careful as you don't want the cheese to burn, so keep an eye on them while they cook.

You can make these balls whatever size you like – if you make them a little smaller they are great for the school lunchbox. Or make them big enough to fit in your pocket for work. Enjoy!

FROG IN THE HOLE

Serves 4

To all my British friends, this one's for you. I've lost count of the number of times I've been told you need an oven to make toad (or frog, as I call it) in the hole. Well, here's my response: an insanely easy and delicious frog in the hole made in the air fryer. Because rules are meant to be broken, right?

GRAB THE FOLLOWING

120 g plain flour

1 teaspoon salt flakes

2 eggs

300 ml milk

olive oil spray

8 mini sausages (preferably pork), scored

TO SERVE

finely sliced red onion (optional)

rosemary sprigs (optional)

HP or tomato sauce

ARE YOU READY?

Place the flour, salt, eggs and half the milk in a large bowl and give it a really good whisk. Gradually add the rest of the milk and keep whisking until the mixture looks silky smooth. Set aside to rest at room temperature for 30 minutes and go put your feet up.

Grease a small round baking dish with olive oil spray and add the mini sausages. Place in the air fryer and cook on 190°C for 5 minutes. When you open the air fryer the smell should be divine. Now pour in the batter and return the dish to the air fryer. Reduce the temperature to 180°C and cook for 15 minutes or until the batter is golden brown and the sausages are perfectly cooked.

Top with some sliced red onion and rosemary, if you like. If you're missing the UK, serve with HP sauce; otherwise, crack open the tomato sauce and enjoy.

EXTRA, EXTRA, READ ALL ABOUT IT!

You could also use four small ramekins to make this dish, so that everybody gets their own individual frog!

Frog in the hole is also served with a simple gravy, which is totally fine, but try to avoid using packet gravy if you can. A little stock, veggies, flour and some wine and you have yourself the most awesome homemade gravy. Peace out.

KIFFLI

Makes about 10

Kiffli are Macedonian pastries that are similar to French croissants, but are made in a fraction of the time as Macedonians don't like to spend three days waiting for food. They make an amazing addition to school lunchboxes, plus my mum would freak out if I didn't include the recipe in this book. So, here is my simplified air-fryer version of the Macedonian croissant.

YOU'LL NEED

150 g (1 cup) self-raising flour

185 g (¾ cup) natural yoghurt, plus extra to serve (optional)

75 g ricotta

1 egg, lightly beaten

1 tablespoon sesame seeds

LET'S ROCK IT LIKE THIS

Place the flour and yoghurt in a blender, push the button and sing the intro to Pearl Jam's 'Better Man', which is about 1 minute. In that time the ingredients will have transformed into a dough and you are ready to go. Divide the dough into six even-sized balls.

Flatten each dough ball into a 5 mm thick disc, then, using a sharp knife, cut a large triangle from each disc using the full length of the dough. Re-roll the leftover dough and cut out as many triangles as you can. Nothing goes to waste.

Place 1 teaspoon of ricotta in the middle of each triangle and roll up from the base of the triangle, like you would a croissant, trapping the ricotta in the dough.

Brush your triangles with the beaten egg, then sprinkle the sesame seeds on top. Line the base of your air fryer with baking paper and pop the kiffli in. Cook on 180°C for 6 minutes. I know, right, only 6 minutes – crazy!

Enjoy the kiffli hot, with some yoghurt for dipping if you like, or let them cool and add them to lunchboxes. If you are going to eat them at work, explain how you made them from scratch to show what a legend you are.

 EXTRA FUN STUFF

You don't have to use ricotta; sometimes I make them plain or I'll use a different cheese or even salami. There are no rules when it comes to my recipes, it's about making them your own because you rock!

CRISPY, CHEESY FILO PASTRY

Makes 1 small pastry

When I was a kid many, many years ago, my mum used to spend hours in the kitchen making a traditional Macedonian dish called 'maznik'. I remember it being delicious, but when I recently asked my mum for the recipe I almost fell over when I saw just how complicated it was. I had to simplify it as there was no chance of me making the filo from scratch. I found frozen filo pastry in the supermarket and my new creation was born.

YOU WILL NEED

1 sheet of frozen filo pastry, just thawed

125 g (½ cup) ricotta

1 egg, lightly beaten

1 teaspoon sesame seeds

LET'S GET CRACKING

The filo pastry is very fragile and paper thin, so be gentle with it. Lay the filo on your work surface or a large chopping board with the long edge facing you. Spoon the ricotta onto the filo and spread it out, leaving a 4 cm border around the edges. Don't be shy with the ricotta, you can load it up.

Now for the fun part: fold in the left and right edges of the filo pastry and prepare to roll. Using the palms of your hands, start rolling the pastry away from you, enclosing the ricotta. Be gentle, but make sure you roll it up quite tightly to create a long ricotta roll.

The final stage is about to rock, so grab one end of your ricotta roll and start rolling it into itself to create a small snail.

Line a baking tray that will fit in your air fryer with baking paper and pop the pastry on the tray. Brush with the beaten egg and sprinkle over the sesame seeds. Cook on 160°C for 8 minutes, after which time it should be golden brown and looking mighty fine. You can eat it immediately or pop it in the school lunchbox.

COOL TIPS

The beauty of this dish is that you can double or triple the quantities and add more rolls to your filo snail to make it as big as you want. Or simply make multiple smaller snails as I have done here.

The ricotta is lovely and mild, but if you want some bite, try feta instead. Or imagine filling these with grated apple and cinnamon. OMG!

PUFF DADDY DAWGS

Makes 12

Okay, so I'm gangsta ... I thought you should know that. I don't make these 'dawgs' for the lunchbox as I don't like the girls eating processed meat too often, but they are great for parties (and not just kids' parties – these bad boys are the ultimate finger food for adults!). I blew my own mind the first time I made them as not only are they inexpensive, but they look amazing and taste incredible.

GO GRAB THIS STUFF

12 mini frankfurts

2 sheets of frozen puff pastry, just thawed

6 slices of cheddar, cut in half

1 egg, lightly beaten

1 teaspoon sesame seeds

TO SERVE

tomato sauce

mustard

NOW DO THIS

Parboil the mini frankfurts – whatever the packet says, just cook them for half the amount of time. So, if it says boil the mini frankfurts for 6 minutes, boil them for 3 minutes. (I worked that out without a calculator.)

While the frankfurts are boiling away, grab your pastry sheets and cut them in half, then cut each half into thirds so you have twelve rectangles.

Place half a slice of cheddar and a mini frankfurt at the base of one of the pastry rectangles, then roll it up and secure the pastry, preferably with the join at the top. Now make the rest of the dawgs with the remaining pastry, cheddar and frankfurts. Using a pastry brush, brush the tops with the beaten egg and sprinkle over the sesame seeds.

Line the base of your air fryer with baking paper and pop the dawgs straight in. Cook on 175°C for 10 minutes or until they are puffed and golden.

Meanwhile, grab a platter and a couple of small serving bowls. Fill one bowl with tomato sauce and the other with mustard – the kids will be dipping their Puff Daddy dawgs into them. Arrange the dawgs on the platter, grab a handful of napkins and party on!

NEXT-LEVEL GARLIC AND TOMATO FOCACCIA

Makes 2

This focaccia is so easy and fancy pantsy. I have made it as a dinner for one and have also served it as a pre-dinner snack for friends. I mean, seriously, do you need an excuse to make garlic and tomato focaccia?

GO GRAB THIS STUFF

150 g (1 cup) self-raising flour, plus extra for dusting

250 g (1 cup) natural yoghurt

2 tablespoons olive oil

2 garlic cloves

pinch of salt flakes

12–14 cherry tomatoes on the vine

rosemary sprigs with flowers, to serve (optional)

WHAT'S NEXT?

Grab a stand mixer with the dough hook attached or a mixing bowl, add the flour and yoghurt and mix or stir until a dough forms. Tip the dough onto a lightly floured work surface and knead for about 5 minutes or until it's smooth and awesome looking. Divide the dough into two balls, cover with plastic wrap and leave to rest for 10–15 minutes.

Pour the olive oil into a small bowl and, using a microplane or the fine side of a box grater, grate the garlic directly into the olive oil. Add the salt, stir well and set aside. (I've always wanted to say 'set aside' – it makes me feel like a proper chef dude.)

Grab some baking paper and one of your rested dough thingies and use your hands to flatten the dough out on the baking paper to a size that will fit in your air fryer, remembering that it will puff up a little when cooking (just like I do when I eat four of these bad boys). You can also use a rolling pin to do this.

Brush half the olive oil mixture over the flattened dough, making sure you brush some of the garlic over as well, and top with half the cherry tomatoes. Lift up the baking paper and pop the whole thing in the air fryer to cook on 175°C for 9 minutes. While it's cooking, prepare the second focaccia with the remaining ingredients.

Top with some rosemary, if you like, then slice as you would a pizza if you're going to share, or just sit in front of the TV and demolish them yourself.

BONUS AWESOMENESS

This focaccia is also delicious topped with basil leaves.

I love the look of the vined tomatoes sitting whole on the focaccia, so I leave the vine attached until my guests say, 'OMG, that looks amazing', then I remove the vine and slice the focaccia.

PANZEROTTI

Makes 3

When I was young, I used to play soccer for an all-Italian team with my best mate Alex. When we first joined Puglia F.C. we had no idea that we would come for the soccer but stay for the panzerotti. 'What are panzerotti?' I hear you ask. Well, they are small, fried Italian calzones stuffed with different ingredients, such as passata, anchovies, basil and mozzarella, and they were the reason we won the league. This version of panzerotti is a little healthier, as I use puff pastry for flakiness rather than the traditional thicker dough.

GRAB THE FOLLOWING

450 g passata or pizza sauce

3 sheets of frozen puff pastry, just thawed

2 balls of buffalo mozzarella, roughly torn

9 anchovy fillets

1 egg, lightly beaten

1 teaspoon salt flakes (optional)

1 basil sprig, leaves picked

ARE YOU READY?

Normally, panzerotti are small but we are going to make these big enough to share (or perhaps not share). Spoon 3 tablespoons of the passata or pizza sauce in the centre of each pastry sheet and spread it out, leaving a 3 cm border. Top with the mozzarella and the anchovy fillets (don't worry if they are oily as this adds the flavour we are looking for).

Fold each sheet of pastry over the filling to make a triangle, then tuck the corners underneath to make a rough-looking semicircle. Press down firmly to seal the pastry or crimp with a fork if you want fancy pastry marks, but I love the rustic Italian approach.

Using a pastry brush, channel Michelangelo and paint the beaten egg over the top of the panzerotti, then sprinkle over the salt, if using. Line the base of your air fryer with baking paper and cook the panzerotti one at a time on 170°C for 12 minutes or until golden brown.

Serve the panzerotti on a board with the basil leaves scattered over the top.

OTHER COOL STUFF

You can add meat to your panzerotti – Italian sausage or ham would be awesome.

Just picture wrapping a napkin around one of these bad boys and giving it to the kids to take outside and run amok. Making food that allows you to kick everyone out of the house is a definite bonus.

ROCKIN' CEVAPI ROLLS

Makes 16

This recipe is a cross between a beef Wellington and an Aussie sausage roll. Any kid from the Balkans will tell you that cevapi (also called kebabi) are the best. They're like sausages, but without the skin, and they're usually made with pork and beef mince. You can buy them at most supermarkets these days, which is a good thing.

I decided to incorporate this delicious meat in an Aussie way to bring these two cultures together between layers of flaky puff pastry. Let's do this!

YOU WILL NEED

16 cevapi (see Cool Tips)

2 tablespoons olive oil

1 tablespoon salt flakes

1 tablespoon garlic powder

2 sheets of frozen puff pastry, just thawed

1 egg, lightly beaten

100 g ajvar (see Cool Tips)

NOW DO THIS

I have been cooking cevapi for at least 35 years, and I've never changed the recipe because it's something you just don't mess with. Place the cevapi in a baking dish that will fit in your air fryer, then drizzle over the olive oil and sprinkle with the salt and garlic powder. Using tongs, move the cevapi around so they are coated in the mixture, then transfer the dish to your air fryer and cook on 180°C for 5 minutes.

Meanwhile, cut each puff pastry sheet into quarters, then cut each quarter in half. You should end up with sixteen rectangles in total. Remove the cevapi from the air fryer and allow them to cool a little – they will release moisture and this will prevent the puff pastry from getting soggy.

Place one cevapi on top of each pastry rectangle. Roll them up to encase the cevapi in pastry, then tuck in the ends to secure. Brush the rolls with the beaten egg, then pop them back in the baking dish in the air fryer and cook for 8 minutes or until the pastry is puffed up and golden brown.

Once the cevapi rolls are ready, transfer to a wooden board. Pop the ajvar in a small bowl or ramekin and serve alongside the rolls. Enjoy!

COOL TIPS

I love buying my cevapi from my local butcher, as they're always fresh and made with love. Take the time to find the best cevapi and I promise you it will be worth it.

Ajvar is an Eastern European capsicum relish that can be mild or spicy. It is available at most supermarkets.

Chips, dips, nachos, ribs and
other awesome (and guilt-free!) snacks

BAR SNACKS

FOR WHEN YOU'RE NOWHERE NEAR A BAR

SWEET POTATO CHIPS WITH SMOKED PAPRIKA DIP

Serves 2–4

Feeling like a guilt-free snack? Yep, me too. Check out these simple sweet potato chips that, allegedly, make a rocking beer snack as well as being the perfect accompaniment to a chilled bottle of Prosecco. The dip is truly awesome and you can use it as a sauce in other recipes, such as the smokin' fish tacos on page 103.

such as the smokin' fish tacos on page 103.

YOU WILL NEED

1 large sweet potato

olive oil spray

1 teaspoon salt flakes

SMOKED PAPRIKA DIP

125 g (½ cup) natural yoghurt

1 teaspoon smoked paprika, plus extra if you like

WHAT'S NEXT?

The first question is, to peel or not to peel the sweet potato? Don't peel! All the nutrients are in the skin, so leave it alone. Grab a sharp knife and slice the sweet potato into chips about the width of your little finger.

Line the base of your air fryer with baking paper and add the chips. Spray them with olive oil and sprinkle over the salt, then cook on 185°C for 15 minutes or until golden and crispy.

Now, while these bad boys are cooking, let's make the delicious dip. Grab a bowl and add the natural yoghurt and smoked paprika. Stir until combined, tasting as you go and adding more smoked paprika if you like. If you have added too much, you can always add more yoghurt to dilute the smoked paprika.

Tip the sweet potato chips into a basket and let them cool for a minute or two, then add the dip in a fancy way so it looks cool. Grab a drink and enjoy!

 COOL TIPS

If you want to spice things up, add ½ teaspoon of cayenne pepper to the dip.

If you're not a dip type of person, you can sprinkle smoked paprika over the chips just after you've coated them with olive oil and salt. I recommend serving the chips with extra salt flakes to give them more bang.

Serving these chips in a paper cone drizzled with my legendary smoked paprika dip is a great suggestion. Remember, sharing is caring, but not when it comes to these.

CHILLI ONION RINGS

Serves 4

You can make these onion rings without the chilli, but I like to add extra so that no one else dares eat them and there's more for me. It's a typical egg wash and breadcrumb situation here, but it's the one per cent spice that makes all the difference. These onion rings make a cool side dish served with the chicken parma on page 112.

YOU WILL NEED

50 g (½ cup) dried breadcrumbs

3 tablespoons grated parmesan

1 tablespoon smoked paprika

1 teaspoon cayenne pepper

1 teaspoon chilli powder

1 teaspoon garlic powder

1 teaspoon celery salt

1 teaspoon freshly ground black pepper

2 eggs, lightly beaten

2 large onions, cut into 1 cm thick rounds, rings separated

olive oil spray

ARE YOU READY?

Place the breadcrumbs, parmesan, smoked paprika, cayenne, chilli powder, garlic powder, celery salt and pepper in a shallow bowl and mix well with a fork.

Place the beaten egg in a separate shallow bowl.

Line the base of your air fryer with baking paper.

Dip the onion rings in the beaten egg, then straight into the breadcrumb mixture, then straight into the air fryer. When the air fryer is choc-a-block full, spray the onion rings with olive oil to coat well.

Turn the air fryer to 200°C and cook for 6 minutes or until golden brown and crispy. These onion rings make the perfect side dish or the ultimate dude food. Enjoy!

 COOL TIPS

If you want to reduce the level of spice, leave out the cayenne pepper and chilli powder, but leave in the smoked paprika as this gives the onion rings the smokiness they need to make them authentic and delicious.

On a side note, I've only recently gotten into celery salt. If you don't like it, feel free to use regular salt flakes instead.

GUILT-FREE NASHVILLE FRIED CHICKEN

Serves 4 (or 1 if you're me)

I love southern-style fried chicken. It's so good (I kept telling my wife) that I had to perfect it, so I just kept making and enjoying it. But the truth is, this recipe took the longest to get right in the air fryer. It needed to be absolutely perfect and it ended up on the cover, too. It's the crunchiest, most delicious (and guilt-free) southern-style hot chicken you are ever going to eat.

GO GRAB THIS STUFF

90 g (3 cups) cornflakes

75 g (½ cup) plain flour

90 g (½ cup) rice flour

1 tablespoon cayenne pepper

1 tablespoon salt flakes

1 tablespoon garlic powder

3 tablespoons smoked paprika

1 tablespoon onion powder

500 ml (2 cups) buttermilk

8 chicken wings

8 chicken drumsticks

SMOKY SAUCE

3 tablespoons vegetable oil

1 tablespoon smoked paprika

1 teaspoon cayenne pepper

1 teaspoon salt flakes

1 teaspoon garlic powder

TO SERVE

lime cheeks

mayonnaise

coriander leaves

LET'S MAKE THIS!

Crush the cornflakes in a large mixing bowl with your hands.

Grab another mixing bowl and add all the remaining dry ingredients. Give them a whisk, then mix through the buttermilk to create a delicious orange batter.

Line the base of your air fryer with baking paper.

Dip a chicken piece in the batter and use your fingers to make sure it is covered. Let it drain a little so it's not dripping, then place in the cornflakes and press well to make sure it is coated evenly. Pop in the air fryer. Repeat this process until your air fryer is full.

Cook the chicken for 20 minutes on 180°C. Crank the air fryer to 190°C and cook for a further 3–5 minutes until the chicken is cooked through and golden.

While your chicken is cooking, mix the smoky sauce ingredients in a small bowl.

Once your chicken is cooked, transfer it to a tray and brush over the smoky sauce. Serve with some lime cheeks, mayo and coriander.

 COOL TIPS Rolling up your sleeves and getting into it is the best way to eat these – put the fork down as it's fingers only. I like to add some pickles for an extra hit of deliciousness.

You can also use chicken thigh or breast fillets to make the best crumbed chicken burgers.

PORK CRACKLING LETTUCE CUPS

Serves 4

These pork crackling cups were inspired by a trip to Vietnam where I fell in love with banh mi. This is my healthier lunchbox-friendly version – the air-fried crackling is to die for!

YOU'LL NEED ALL THIS

600 g pork belly

2 onions, halved

2 tablespoons salt flakes

2 baby cos lettuces, leaves separated

2 long red chillies, finely sliced

1 Lebanese cucumber, halved lengthways, deseeded and sliced

handful of coriander leaves

3 tablespoons hoisin sauce

NOW DO THIS

This wonderful pork crackling journey starts the night before, or perhaps just a few hours before if you don't have thyme on your hands. No, not that thyme but this time. Using paper towel, dab the pork belly to remove excess moisture – you want the skin to be as dry as possible. Pop it in the fridge overnight or for a few hours to further dry out the skin.

Take the pork out of the fridge 1 hour before cooking so it can come to room temperature, then dab away any remaining moisture. Place the onion halves in an aluminium tray that will fit in your air fryer and place the pork belly, skin-side up, on top of the onion. Use a sharp knife to score the skin diagonally at 1 cm intervals, but don't score the layer of fat underneath. Massage the salt into the skin and the scored cuts.

Place the tray in your air fryer, crank it to maximum heat (240–260°C) and cook for 10–12 minutes. Check it at the 6-minute mark and again at the 10-minute mark to ensure it's not cooking too fast. This first stage is where the magic happens with the crackling – it's like watching popcorn pop.

Once the crackling starts to appear, reduce the temperature to 140°C and cook for another 18 minutes or until the pork is cooked through (the liquid in the tray will be clear). Remove the tray from the air fryer and rest the pork on a heap of paper towel loosely covered with foil for 10 minutes.

Meanwhile, arrange the lettuce, chilli, cucumber and coriander in separate piles on a large wooden serving board. Put the hoisin in a small bowl and pop it on the board, too.

Using a sharp knife, cut along the scored skin of the pork belly, place the pork slices and crackling on the board and invite everyone to load up their lettuce cups.

OTHER COOL STUFF

Roast your favourite vegetables to go with the pork and you have the ultimate Sunday roast.

When I was in Vietnam once, I watched an old lady take the whole pork crackling off the pork belly, turn it over and cook it again, to develop crackling on both sides! Mind blown. If you are going to attempt this, don't score the skin.

DID SOMEONE SAY NACHOS?

Serves 2–4

The secret to these awesome nachos is the salsa and the ever-so-slightly burnt cheese on the corn chips. Oh yes, my mouth is watering already just writing this; in fact, hang on, I'm going to see if I have the ingredients here now so I can make them …

Okay, I'm back. As I was saying, this is seriously good, so let's do it!

GRAB THE FOLLOWING

400 g corn chips

250 g (2 cups) grated cheddar

1 teaspoon smoked paprika

1 largish avocado, mashed

salt flakes and freshly ground
black pepper

chopped coriander leaves,
to serve

BEST EVER SALSA

2 juicy tomatoes, diced

½ red onion, finely chopped

1 bird's eye chilli, finely chopped

1 teaspoon salt flakes

juice of 1 small lime, plus lime
wedges to serve

WHAT'S NEXT?

Grab an ovenproof plate that will perfectly fit in your air fryer and line it with baking paper. Place a single layer of corn chips on the plate and scatter a layer of cheddar over the top. Sprinkle over a pinch of the smoked paprika. Now, add a second layer of corn chips, another layer of cheese and another sprinkle of paprika. Repeat this process until you have six or seven layers. That's right, I don't muck around when it comes to nachos!

Pop the corn chips in the air fryer and cook on 180°C for 5 minutes. This will give you time to make the best ever salsa.

Place the tomato, onion and chilli in a bowl and mix well. Add the salt and lime juice and stir it up, baby. Transfer to a fancy looking serving bowl.

Place the mashed avo in a small bowl and season to taste with salt and pepper.

When the cheese has melted and the corn chips have started to darken, remove from the air fryer and slide onto a wooden board, baking paper and all. Sprinkle with some chopped coriander and serve with the avo, salsa and some lime wedges for squeezing over.

 EXTRA FUN STUFF You can add some sliced grilled chicken to these nachos, but the real hero is the salsa. Enjoy!

'PARTY ON WAYNE' POTATO SKINS

Serves 4

You can't have an air fryer cookbook without a recipe for the best potato skins. I had to eat a lot of potatoes to perfect this dish, so I hope you appreciate the final result. Sometimes the simplest things in life are the best, and this recipe proves it.

GO GRAB THIS STUFF

6 potatoes (I use russet potatoes), halved

2 tablespoons olive oil

1 tablespoon salt flakes

90 g butter

3 short-cut bacon rashers, diced

90 g (¾ cup) grated cheddar

250 g (1 cup) sour cream

3 spring onions, finely sliced

1 tablespoon finely chopped chives

freshly ground black pepper, to serve

LET'S DO THIS

There are two parts to cooking these bad boys, so let's get started. Use a melon baller or teaspoon to remove most of the flesh from each potato half, leaving a 1 cm border. (Don't throw the flesh away – see Extra Fancy Stuff below for a rocking way to use it!) Using a fork, score the inside of each potato half so they're roughed up on the base. Turn the halves over, brush the skins with the olive oil and sprinkle with half the salt.

Line a small baking tray with baking paper and place the potato skins on the tray, face down. No, not your face, the potato face, meaning the skin is facing up. Glad we cleared that up. Pop the tray in the air fryer and cook on 190°C for 5 minutes, then turn the potato halves over and cook for a further 5 minutes.

Take the tray out of the air fryer and place 1 teaspoon of butter in each potato half, then top with the bacon and cheddar. Sprinkle with the remaining salt, then return to the air fryer and cook on 190°C for 30 minutes until golden and crispy.

Remove from the air fryer, dollop on the sour cream and scatter with the spring onion, chives and some pepper. Or, if you prefer, you can put the sour cream in a side dish topped with the chives and invite peeps to add it themselves.

 You can use any potatoes you like for this recipe, even sweet potatoes will work (just remember to change the name to sweet potato skins).

Feel free to add or leave out any ingredients, but I recommend keeping things simple to allow the potato skins to really sing.

Instead of chucking out the potato flesh, toss it with a little olive oil and salt, then pop it in the air fryer for 10 minutes to create the ultimate rustic chips.

STICKY PORK RIBS (AND FINGERS)

Serves 4

When I scroll through my Instagram feed and see someone eating pork ribs, I have to make them. These sticky pork ribs are all about contrasting flavours, spice and, most importantly, the experience. I like to serve them with fresh chilli scattered on top because of the extra kick they give. They are guaranteed, finger-licking awesome.

GO GRAB THIS STUFF

3 tablespoons salt-reduced soy sauce

45 g (¼ cup) brown sugar

90 g (¼ cup) maple syrup

3 tablespoons worcestershire sauce

1 tablespoon garlic powder

1 tablespoon onion powder

2 tablespoons olive oil

750 g rack pork ribs

3 spring onions, finely sliced

2 long red chillies, finely sliced

WHAT'S NEXT?

In a small bowl, place the soy sauce, brown sugar, maple syrup, worcestershire sauce, garlic powder, onion powder and olive oil and stir until really well combined. If you are wondering why there's no salt, it's because the soy sauce and worcestershire sauce are salty enough.

Line the base of your air fryer with baking paper. You can cut the rack of pork ribs into separate ribs to fit more in your air fryer if you like, or leave the rack whole. Pop the ribs on the baking paper and use a pastry brush to brush over three-quarters of the marinade. Cook on 180°C for 5 minutes, then reduce the temperature to 150°C and cook for about 30 minutes. At the 15-minute mark, baste the ribs with half the remaining marinade, then baste again with the remaining marinade about 3 minutes before the ribs are ready.

Remove the ribs from the air fryer and rest on a wooden serving board for about 10 minutes. If no one's watching, have a little nibble – it's called cook's privilege. Now, cut the ribs along the bone to create individual sticky delights. Sprinkle the spring onion and chilli over the top and dig in.

 ALSO TRY THIS! You can serve these ribs as a meal for one or pass them around as finger food. The choice is yours, but eating them with an apple slaw and fries makes them even better.

BACON AND CHICKEN BITES

Makes 10

Picture being at a street carnival somewhere hot, or perhaps hanging out at the beach in Bondi, St Kilda or Surfers Paradise. The smell coming from the street vendors is making you hungry, but it's only 3 pm. What do you do? Run home and make these bacon and chicken bites, of course. Don't mess around with anything else.

GET THE FOLLOWING DELIVERED

2 tablespoons olive oil

1 chicken breast, cut into 10 x 1 cm thick strips

1 teaspoon salt flakes

1 tablespoon garlic powder

3 short-cut bacon rashers, cut lengthways into 10 x 1 cm thick strips

10 cherry tomatoes, plus extra to serve

oregano leaves, to serve (optional)

LET'S MAKE THIS!

Drizzle the olive oil on both sides of the chicken, then sprinkle with the salt flakes and garlic powder. Lay the strips of bacon in front of you and top each strip with a piece of chicken and a cherry tomato. Carefully fold the bacon and chicken over the tomato and secure with a toothpick through the middle. Got it? It might take a few goes to get the first one under control, but once you get the hang of it, you'll be set.

Line the base of your air fryer with baking paper and pop your creations in. Cook on 180°C for 8 minutes or until the chicken is cooked through. The cherry tomatoes will be as hot as a road on a 40-degree day, so be careful. Arrange on a plate and add the extra cherry tomatoes and some oregano leaves, if you like.

Choosing to share these bacon and chicken bites is up to you. I love them so much I'm willing to drop them on the floor just so no one else eats them (and yes, I'd still eat them afterwards). However, for legal reasons I'm not suggesting you do this.

The cherry tomatoes take these bacon and chicken bites to another level, so if you're thinking you won't add them, think again. I guess if you really, really, really don't like cherry tomatoes, you can leave them out and dip the bites into tomato or barbecue sauce instead, but they won't be the same.

These bites are always a hit at parties, but if you want people to go home, serve frozen pies instead. I've got your back!

VEGGIE SPRING ROLLS

Makes 10

This is a simple and fun way to get kids to eat their vegetables. I used to make these spring rolls for Anela and Kiki years ago and I love that I now get to share them with you; however, I'm also going to share my spicy dipping sauce for adults, so that everyone can get in on the fun.

GRAB THIS STUFF

½ onion, finely diced

1 celery stalk, cut into matchsticks

2 carrots, cut into matchsticks

50 g (½ cup) finely diced mushrooms

30 g (¼ cup) finely diced broccoli

40 g (¼ cup) finely diced red capsicum

2 garlic cloves, crushed

95 g (½ cup) cooked rice (optional)

3 tablespoons salt-reduced soy sauce

10 sheets of frozen filo pastry, just thawed

1 egg, lightly beaten

1 teaspoon sesame seeds

1 spring onion, green part only, finely sliced

2 bird's eye chillies, finely sliced

ADULTS-ONLY DIPPING SAUCE

3 tablespoons hoisin sauce

2 tablespoons crushed unsalted peanuts

1 tablespoon sriracha chilli sauce

NOW DO THIS

Place the veggies, garlic and rice (if using) in a bowl and stir through the soy sauce.

Take a sheet of filo pastry and trim one of the long ends so you are left with a square (save the offcuts for another use). Place the filo sheet on your chopping board with one corner facing you, so it looks like a diamond. Using a spoon, place 2 tablespoons of the vegetable mixture in the centre of the filo sheet. Now fold it up, spring-roll style. If you don't know how to do this, pop 'how to wrap a spring roll' into the YouTube search bar – it's a game changer. Repeat with the remaining vegetable mixture and filo sheets until you have ten spring rolls.

Brush the beaten egg over the rolls and sprinkle the sesame seeds on top. Line the base of your air fryer with baking paper and pop your rolls in. Cook on 170°C for 8 minutes.

Now for the sauce. If you're making these rolls for the kids, simply spoon the hoisin sauce into small dipping bowls. If you're making them for grown-ups, combine the dipping sauce ingredients in a bowl, then divide among bowls.

Serve the rolls naked for your little humans or sprinkle the spring onion and chilli over for your adult friends; either way, it's win–win.

EXTRA FANCY STUFF

To make these spring rolls even more delicious, try adding 1 teaspoon each of finely chopped lemongrass, ginger and coriander leaves. Yummo.

The dipping sauce is a simple and traditional one that I discovered on my travels to Vietnam, but you can swap it for soy sauce or even sweet chilli sauce if you prefer.

EASY SWEET POTATO FRITTERS

Makes 8

Back in 2019, I created a super easy fritter recipe and shared it on my social media accounts. It was a huge hit, but I always felt that it needed something extra to make it truly worthy of this cookbook. So, ladies and gentlemen, I present to you my easy sweet potato fritters made in ... drum roll ... egg rings!

YOU WILL NEED

1 large sweet potato, coarsely grated, plus extra if needed

80 g (½ cup) peas (frozen ones are cool)

65 g (⅓ cup) corn kernels (fresh or frozen)

1 teaspoon salt flakes

½ teaspoon freshly ground black pepper

3 tablespoons grated parmesan

½ teaspoon chopped chives

2 eggs, plus an extra egg if needed

olive oil spray

YOGHURT DIP

250 g (1 cup) natural yoghurt

1 teaspoon finely chopped chives

WHAT'S NEXT?

Place the sweet potato, peas, corn, salt, pepper, parmesan, chives and eggs in a large bowl. Using a fork, give the ingredients a really good stir – you will notice the mixture getting thicker and everything will become sticky. If the mixture looks a little dry, simply add another egg; if it looks too wet, add a little more grated sweet potato.

The secret now is to make them look pretty – that's right, pretty. Most fritters have rough edges that usually burn during cooking. To fix this problem, I like to use those metal rings that people use to fry perfectly round eggs. Place four egg rings on a piece of baking paper and spray them with some olive oil to grease them. Add half the sweet potato mixture to the rings. How good do they look? Spray a generous amount of olive oil over the top, then lift up the baking paper and pop them in the air fryer. Cook on 170°C for 10 minutes or until golden brown on top.

While the fritters are cooking, place the yoghurt in a small serving bowl and sprinkle the chives on top.

Carefully remove the egg rings and admire your beautiful fritters. Repeat to make a second batch of fritters, then serve them with the yoghurt dip and you're done!

 You can swap the sweet potato for regular potato if you like, and if you don't like peas and corn, you can use other finely chopped veg, such as capsicum or broccoli. Easy!

DADDY'S FAMOUS CHIPS

Serves 2

I've been making chips for my girls for 10 years and have perfected the recipe over time, so much so that when my girls ask for chips they ask for 'Daddy's famous chips'. The best potatoes for making chips are high in starch and low in moisture, so russet spuds, which include yukon gold and king Edward, are my go to. Although don't stress if you can't get hold of these varieties; at the end of the day, you just need potatoes. There is also one secret ingredient that rocks these chips and gives them a unique flavour, so read on and let's get cracking.

WHAT YOU'LL NEED

4 russet potatoes, peeled and cut into 1.5 cm thick chips

olive oil spray

2 teaspoons salt flakes

1 teaspoon vegetable stock powder (I use Vegeta brand)

tomato sauce and mayonnaise, to serve (optional)

OKAY, GREAT – NOW WHAT?

Bring a large saucepan of generously salted water to the boil and add the chips. Return the water to the boil, then cook the chips for 3 minutes. Drain well and pop the chips on a baking tray that will fit in your air fryer. Leave the chips to cool for 15–20 minutes, then lightly spray with olive oil and sprinkle over the salt.

Transfer the tray to your air fryer and cook on 160°C for 6 minutes, then crank the heat up to 200°C and cook for another 2 minutes. We want the chips to have a soft centre and a crisp outer shell.

Pop the chips in a basket or bowl and sprinkle over the vegetable stock powder (it's a little like chicken salt, but with a unique flavour that the kids love). Serve as is or with some tomato sauce and mayo for dipping.

BONUS AWESOMENESS

By cooking the chips twice, we're creating extra crunch. Chef dudes like Heston cook them three times and freeze them in between, but we don't have time for that. Feel free to leave the skin on the potatoes if you prefer, and cut them into wedges or even thin chips. You do you.

SATURDAY PARMESAN OMELETTE

Serves 2–4

This dish is a cross between an omelette and a quiche, but way cooler than either. It's super easy to put together and too delicious to only make on the weekends, so don't let the title fool you. It has an amazing tang, as I use parmesan instead of soft cheese, but you can add whichever cheese you like (just don't tell me, okay?).

GO GRAB THIS STUFF

4 eggs

100 g cherry tomatoes, halved

50 g (½ cup) grated parmesan

2 tablespoons melted butter

½ onion, finely chopped

1 garlic clove, finely chopped

1 teaspoon salt flakes

1 teaspoon freshly ground black pepper

olive oil spray

1 chorizo sausage, sliced

basil leaves, to serve

olive oil, for drizzling

buttered crusty bread, to serve

ARE YOU READY?

Combine the eggs, tomatoes, parmesan, butter, onion, garlic, salt and pepper in a bowl. Give everything a really good stir until the ingredients are well combined.

Grease a small round baking dish with olive oil spray and pour in the egg mixture (or you can divide the mixture among four 10 cm diameter ramekins). Place the chorizo slices on top so they look cool (as they cook their flavour will be absorbed into the omelette).

Place the dish in your air fryer and cook on 170°C for 6 minutes, checking at the halfway mark to make sure the omelette is cooking evenly.

Remove the dish from the air fryer, scatter a few basil leaves over the top and drizzle with olive oil. Serve with the buttered bread and enjoy Saturday every day of the week.

EXTRA, EXTRA, READ ALL ABOUT IT!

Feel free to swap the chorizo for prosciutto or bacon. You can also go nuts with vegetables, such as chopped eggplant, zucchini and asparagus. Simply place the veg in a heatproof bowl, then cover with boiling water for 1 minute. Drain and fold through the egg mixture. If you're like me and enjoy spice, add a few chilli flakes for some serious bang.

CRAZY NOODLE VEGGIES

Serves 4

This idea came to me after I watched a TV commercial of a kid eating soggy noodles with over-cooked vegetables. I thought, what?! Kids want crunchy, not sloppy! So this recipe was born. Intrigued? Good, read on. The idea is to use the air fryer in a non-conventional way to add crunch to delicious veggies. Because why not?

YOU'LL NEED ALL THIS

1 packet of 2-minute noodles

2 small carrots, quartered lengthways

2 broccoli florets

1 small zucchini, quartered lengthways

1 small eggplant, quartered lengthways

1 small red capsicum, quartered lengthways

1 teaspoon salt flakes

1 tablespoon olive oil

TO SERVE (OPTIONAL)

tomato sauce

natural yoghurt

your favourite spicy dipping sauce

NOW WHAT?

Firstly, pop the 2-minute noodles (don't break them up) in a heatproof bowl and pour in enough boiling water to just cover them. Set aside for 1 minute only. Do not add any of the additives from the packet.

Parboil the veggies in a saucepan of boiling water for 3 minutes, then transfer to a large bowl. Add the salt and olive oil and toss to combine.

Drain the noodles and return them to the heatproof bowl. Pick up a long strand of noodles and wrap it around one of the vegetable pieces, almost like the ancient Egyptians did with their mummies. Repeat until the veggie piece is nicely covered in noodles, then set aside and do the same thing for the remaining vegetables and noodles.

Line the base of your air fryer with baking paper and pop the noodle-wrapped veggies in. Cook on 175°C for 5 minutes. We want to give the veggies colour and crunch to encourage our little humans to eat them.

Allow the crazy noodle veggies to cool a little before you feed the troops. Serve with a sprinkle of salt and bowls of tomato sauce or natural yoghurt for dipping, if you like. If adults are going to be eating these too, you could also serve them with a spicy dipping sauce, such as Vietnamese nuoc mam.

EXTRA FUN STUFF

Kids can be the harshest critics and the fussiest ones will often refuse food without explanation, so the purpose of this dish is to dress up veggies by adding some crunch and making them look fun.

You can use any vegetables, or even fruit. Try wrapping slices of pineapple or bananas in noodles (increase the cooking time to 8 minutes) and sprinkling icing sugar on top. Bang!

OMG CHICKEN!
(AKA DAD-STYLE CHICKEN)

Serves 2–3

I'm a total lover of any sort of food where you have to lick your fingers afterwards. This is a finely tuned recipe that I hope you will make over and over for your family and friends. If you are vegetarian, try this recipe using cauliflower instead.

YOU'LL NEED ALL THIS

500 g chicken wings and/or drumettes

2 tablespoons vegetable oil

3 tablespoons honey

125 ml (½ cup) salt-reduced soy sauce

2 tablespoons sriracha chilli sauce (or any other chilli sauce)

1 cm piece of ginger, grated

2 garlic cloves, crushed

TO SERVE

1 teaspoon sesame seeds

2 long red chillies, finely sliced

3 tablespoons finely sliced spring onion

LET'S ROCK IT LIKE THIS

Pat the chicken dry with paper towel, then place it in a bowl. Drizzle the vegetable oil over the top and mix well with your hands to make sure the chicken is evenly coated.

Now for the sticky stuff. Drizzle the honey over the chicken and either use your hands or tongs to coat the chicken (don't stress too much about the honey being even). Add the soy sauce, sriracha chilli sauce, ginger and garlic and mix it all well.

Line a baking tray that will fit in your air fryer with baking paper. Place the chicken on the tray, transfer to the air fryer and cook on 190°C for 6 minutes. Using tongs, turn the chicken over (be careful as the sauce will be very hot), reduce the temperature to 180°C and cook for a further 8 minutes or until the chicken is cooked through.

Sprinkle the sesame seeds over the top, followed by the chilli and spring onion. Eat the chicken while it's hot and enjoy the sweetness of the honey alongside the heat of the chilli.

 COOL TIPS **This chicken is quite spicy, so try serving it with a nice 'cooling-down' bowl of yoghurt; otherwise, eat it au naturel like I do and go through a whole box of tissues while pretending you can handle the heat. If you are making this for little humans, just remove the hot stuff.**

Pasta bakes, burgers, roasts, salads and skewers that are so good they will knock your socks off (so make sure you have a spare pair of socks)

DINNERS THAT WILL WIN YOU

WIN YOU

'PARENT OF THE YEAR'

THE BURGER WITH THE LOT

Makes 6

What makes a great burger? What is the perfect combination? This burger is crazy good, and I say crazy good because it is a little crazy. If you are reading this thinking 'no way', trust me. If you are going to try just one recipe from this awesome book, you have to try this one.

GET THE FOLLOWING DELIVERED

large handful of plain corn chips

250 g good-quality beef mince

250 g good-quality pork mince

1 egg

1 white onion, finely chopped

1 teaspoon salt flakes

1 teaspoon freshly ground black pepper

1 teaspoon garlic powder

12 slices of American (or Australian) cheddar

olive oil spray

TO SERVE

6 soft burger buns, cut in half

mayonnaise

American smoky mustard

6 large lettuce leaves

1 tomato, cut into 5 mm thick slices

6 dill pickles, cut lengthways into 5 mm thick slices, plus extra to serve (optional)

tomato sauce

Daddy's Famous Chips (see page 77)

LET'S ROCK IT LIKE THIS

Place the corn chips in a zip-lock bag, then secure and proceed to let off some steam by smashing up the chips into 5 mm–1 cm pieces.

Place both types of mince, the corn chips, egg, half the onion, the salt, pepper and garlic powder in a large mixing bowl. Using clean hands, mix well to make sure everything is combined. This should take about 5 minutes. Divide the mixture into six even portions and roll them into meatballs. Place the meatballs on a plate and pop them in the fridge for about 20 minutes.

Remove the meatballs from the fridge and let them come to room temperature. Preheat your air fryer on 180°C for 5 minutes.

Working with one meatball at a time, place it between two sheets of baking paper and squash it down until it's about 1 cm thick. Repeat with the remaining meatballs. Line the base of your air fryer with baking paper, pop the patties in and spray with olive oil. Cook for 14 minutes, then place two cheese slices on top of each patty and cook for another 60 seconds – we want the cheese to be perfectly melted.

Grab your buns – no, not those buns, I mean the bread buns. Spread some mayo on the top and bottom half of each bun, followed by some mustard. Sprinkle the remaining onion over the top, add a lettuce leaf, a slice or two of tomato and your cheesy patty. Add some pickle, a squeeze of tomato sauce and the top half of the bun. If you want to impress, use a bamboo skewer to add an extra pickle on top. Serve with my famous chips. You're welcome.

MORE THINGS Feel free to swap out any of the fresh ingredients, but when it comes to the patty I find it's perfect the way it is. The secret ingredient is the corn chips, which add crunch. The 50/50 balance of beef and pork mince ensures there is enough fat in the patty as an all-beef patty can be dry.

These burgers are also great with my sweet potato chips and smoked paprika dip (see page 56).

LAMB KEBABS WITH FLATBREADS

Serves 6

This recipe is unbelievably good. We make these lamb kebabs weekly at home and Kiki absolutely adores them. The lamb and rosemary will knock your socks off, so make sure you have a spare pair handy. We are also going to make our own kid-friendly tzatziki and easy flatbreads, so let's get to it.

YOU'LL NEED ALL THIS

6 lamb cutlets

1 teaspoon salt flakes

2 rosemary sprigs, leaves picked, plus extra sprigs to serve (optional)

¼ small lemon

olive oil spray

½ red onion, finely sliced

1 tomato, cut into wedges

50 g (1 cup) shredded lettuce

TZATZIKI

1 Lebanese cucumber

200 g natural yoghurt

¼ small lemon

1 teaspoon olive oil

½ teaspoon salt flakes

1 garlic clove

EASY FLATBREADS

500 g (3⅓ cups) plain flour, plus extra for dusting

300 g natural yoghurt

½ teaspoon salt flakes

olive oil spray

ARE YOU READY?

Firstly, let's marinate the lamb cutlets so they can chill out in the fridge. Grab a bowl and toss in the lamb cutlets. Add the salt and rosemary leaves, squeeze in the lemon juice and coat the cutlets with olive oil spray. Mix well, then cover with plastic wrap and pop it in the fridge.

To make the tzatziki, grate the cucumber onto a few sheets of paper towel, skin and all. Roll up the paper towel and squeeze out the moisture, then place the cucumber in a bowl, along with the yoghurt. Squeeze in the lemon juice and add the olive oil and salt. If you've got one of those microplanes, grab it now; otherwise, use a box grater to grate the garlic into the bowl and mix well. Cover with plastic wrap and set aside in the fridge.

Line the base of your air fryer with baking paper and put the lamb cutlets in. Cook for 8 minutes on 180°C.

Meanwhile, make the flatbreads. Grab your blender or food processor, add the flour, yoghurt and salt and blitz for 60 seconds or until a dough forms. Transfer the dough to a floured work surface and divide it into six even portions. Working with one portion at a time, flatten the dough using your hands or a rolling pin until it is about 1 cm thick. Continue with the remaining dough to make six flatbreads.

Remove the lamb cutlets from the air fryer and set aside to rest. Meanwhile, cook the flatbreads, two at a time, in the air fryer on 180°C for 4 minutes.

Place the onion, tomato and lettuce in small piles on a serving board. Slice the lamb cutlets and add them to the board, along with the tzatziki, flatbreads and extra rosemary for sprinkling over, if you like. Now start assembling the most delicious lamb kebabs ever.

You can substitute the lamb for any other meat or even tofu. You can omit any ingredient you like; for example, the raw garlic in the tzatziki is a little too much for some. You can also make it spicy by adding a drizzle of sriracha chilli sauce.

TAVCHE GRAVCHE

Serves 2

This recipe is very dear to me – it's what I ate as a kid at least once a week, and over the years it has become my comfort soul food. My mum would spend hours in the kitchen preparing tavche gravche, which is similar to the French dish cassoulet. The good news is that I have simplified my mum's recipe so you can whip it up any night of the week. The way you say 'tavche gravche' is 'taa-vv-che gra-vv-che'. Okay, now you're officially Macedonian, so let's make this.

GRAB THE FOLLOWING

2 x 400 g cans cannellini beans

1 tablespoon olive oil

2 onions, 1 finely chopped, 1 cut into 1 cm thick rounds

4 garlic cloves, crushed

2 teaspoons salt flakes

2 tablespoons smoked paprika

1 teaspoon dried mint

1 chorizo or Italian sausage, cut in half lengthways and scored

2 bird's eye chillies

mint leaves, to serve

crusty bread, to serve

LET'S DO THIS!

I love using individual ramekins for this dish as they look super cool. Even better, if you have an old-school clay dish use it instead, as this is the way my mum used to make it. Crack open the cans of beans and pour out most of the liquid but don't completely drain them. Pour the beans into two 500 ml (2 cup) capacity ramekins or one larger round baking dish.

Heat the olive oil in a frying pan over medium heat, add the finely chopped onion, garlic, half the salt and half the smoked paprika and sauté for 6–8 minutes until the onion is translucent. Add the onion and garlic mixture to the beans and stir well. Add 125 ml (½ cup) of water to each ramekin or 250 ml (1 cup) of water to the dish, then stir through the dried mint and the remaining salt and smoked paprika. Now grab the onion rounds and pop them on top, gently pushing down so they're level with the beans. Place the sausage halves and chillies on top of the beans.

Pop the ramekins or dish in the air fryer and cook on 175°C for 20 minutes. We are looking for a crust to form over the beans without drying them out, so check the ramekins or dish a few times towards the end of the cooking time.

Scatter some mint leaves over the top and serve straight away with some crusty bread, if you like. I would love to know what you think of this dish – if you make it please take a snap and post it to my Insta handle.

BONUS AWESOMENESS

I remember eating this with thick slices of crusty Vienna bread as a kid. I'd dip the bread into the dish to soak up the delicious sauce.

If you're vegetarian or vegan, just add rounds of eggplant instead of the sausage. You can also swap the sausage for pork ribs or beef patties. There are no rules, so make it your own and share the love with your family at dinnertime.

PIZZA TO DIE FOR

Makes 2 mini pizzas

A good mate of mine owns the best pizzeria I've ever been to, and I am so fortunate that he gave me a pizza lesson to treasure. A huge shout-out to my friend Adamo from Pizzeria Adamo in my hometown Geelong, who was super kind in sharing his love for authentic Italian cooking.

When I was in Italy last year, I discovered that when it comes to pizza, Italians are all about a few quality toppings rather than a 'burger with the lot' approach, so I've kept it simple here. The dough makes eight bases, so freeze the leftovers and take them out the night before your next pizza session.

WHAT YOU'LL NEED

2 x 7 g sachets dried yeast

1 teaspoon sugar

620 ml warm water

1 kg bread flour, plus extra for dusting

1 teaspoon salt flakes

2 tablespoons tomato pizza sauce or passata

1 ball of buffalo mozzarella, roughly torn

15 slices of good-quality Italian salami

1 basil sprig, leaves picked

1 teaspoon extra-virgin olive oil

THIS IS HOW WE DO IT

Grab a jug and add the yeast, sugar and warm water. Let it sit for about 30 minutes – the sugar and heat will activate the yeast and it will look like a cappuccino with the froth on top.

Place the flour and salt in a stand mixer with the dough hook attached and briefly combine. Turn the mixer to low and add half the yeast mixture, keeping an eye on it so it picks up your positive vibes (okay, not true, but make sure the flour doesn't stick to the base of the bowl). Gradually add the rest of the yeast mixture. The dough may seem a little wet but, trust me, the Italians swear by a wetter dough. Mix for about 8 minutes or until smooth, then tip onto a lightly floured work surface and knead for another minute or so. Place the dough in a lightly oiled bowl, cover with plastic wrap and leave to rise at room temperature for 2 hours or until doubled in size.

Line a baking tray that will fit in your air fryer with baking paper.

Once the dough has risen, divide it into eight even-sized portions. Dust your bench with flour, add a ball of dough and start stretching it out by hand. Using your fingers, push out the dough until it's the size of the prepared tray. Lift the dough onto the tray, then add 1 tablespoon of pizza sauce or passata and spread it evenly over the dough. Dot half the mozzarella over top, then scatter over half the salami.

Pop the pizza straight into the air fryer for 4 minutes on maximum heat. Meanwhile, make a second pizza with the remaining ingredients and pop the leftover dough portions into separate zip-lock bags and put them in the freezer.

Once the cheese is melted and the base is cooked, remove the pizza and pop it on a board. Top with half the basil and drizzle over half the olive oil. Repeat with the second pizza.

BONUS AWESOMENESS

The pizza base is non-negotiable, the only thing I'm willing to negotiate on here are the toppings. This easy and fun recipe is designed to get your little humans involved in cooking.

VEGETARIAN MOUSSAKA

Serves 4

This is a modified moussaka for the new-age hipster. Made in ramekins to perfectly fit in the air fryer, it breaks all the rules. When traditional dishes such as moussaka were invented back in the day, they didn't take into consideration that we'd post pictures of them all over social media, making us even busier than we already are. This recipe brings moussaka into the crazy modern world we now live in, so buckle up and start your engines.

GET THE FOLLOWING DELIVERED

3 tablespoons olive oil

2 onions, finely chopped

2 garlic cloves, crushed

2 teaspoons salt flakes

500 g mushrooms, roughly chopped

400 g can diced tomatoes

1 teaspoon freshly ground
black pepper

5 potatoes, peeled and cut into
5 mm thick rounds

2 zucchini, cut into 5 mm
thick rounds

50 g (½ cup) grated parmesan

chopped oregano or flat-leaf
parsley leaves, to serve

BECHAMEL

600 ml light thickened cream

1 egg, lightly beaten

150 g (1½ cups) grated parmesan

2 tablespoons cornflour

LET'S DO THIS!

You can either make the moussaka filling directly in your air fryer or you can use a baking dish. Pour in the olive oil, add the onion, garlic and half the salt and cook in the air fryer on 170°C for 4 minutes. Add the mushroom, tomatoes, pepper and remaining salt, then stir well and cook for 5 minutes.

To make the bechamel, grab a small saucepan and add the cream, egg and parmesan. Place over medium heat and stir until the parmesan has melted, then add the cornflour and cook, stirring constantly, for 4–5 minutes, until the sauce thickens. Remove from the heat and set aside.

It's time to assemble, so grab four 300 ml capacity ramekins and grease the insides with olive oil. Cover the base of each ramekin with a layer of potato, followed by a layer of zucchini. Add 1 tablespoon of the mushroom mixture followed by a tablespoon of bechamel. Repeat the process until you can fit no more in, but make sure you finish with a layer of potato. You've done well! Sprinkle the parmesan over the top – as it melts it will create a crusty, golden cheese crackling. Transfer the ramekins to the air fryer and cook on 170°C for 18 minutes or until cooked through.

Top the moussakas with some oregano or parsley and serve.

If you are a meat lover, you can swap the mushrooms for the same quantity of beef or chicken mince. You might have to season the dish a little more, but be careful as the parmesan is obviously salty.

I find that the ramekins make the perfect-sized moussaka for my girls at dinnertime – they might look small but the moussaka is very filling.

MAC 'N' CHEESE

Serves 4

Have you ever read the ingredients label on a packet of frozen mac 'n' cheese? If you haven't, don't do it, just read and make this recipe instead. Mac 'n' cheese has become super trendy in recent years, with the boom in popularity of Southern US cuisine, moving from the perfect side dish to the main event. Let's get this show on the road.

YOU'LL NEED ALL THIS

300 g dried penne

75 g butter

80 g fresh breadcrumbs

3 tablespoons plain flour

1 teaspoon mustard powder

1 teaspoon smoked paprika

300 ml warm milk

150 g grated cheddar

100 g buffalo mozzarella, roughly torn

50 g (½ cup) grated parmesan

finely chopped chives, to serve

NOW DO THIS

Firstly, cook the penne in a saucepan of salted boiling water for 3 minutes. Drain the pasta and transfer to a round baking dish that will fit in your air fryer.

Melt half the butter in a small saucepan over medium heat, then add the breadcrumbs and stir well. Turn off the heat and let the mixture cool a little.

Place a large saucepan over medium heat and add the rest of the butter. Let it melt, then add the flour and stir for about 20 seconds. Sprinkle in the mustard powder and smoked paprika, then remove from the heat and add the milk while stirring constantly. Return to medium heat and slowly bring the mixture to the boil – take your time and enjoy the process, watching as it gradually thickens. After a couple of minutes, add the cheddar and stir until it melts, then stir through the mozzarella.

Pour the oozing cheese sauce over the penne and sprinkle the buttery breadcrumbs and parmesan over the top. Once everything is in, transfer the dish to your air fryer, crank it to 180°C and cook for 15 minutes. This will look (and taste) absolutely to die for, so all you need to do now is scatter over some chives and serve.

COOL TIPS

You can serve the mac 'n' cheese with a salad of green leaves and cherry tomatoes. Make a simple dressing by combining 3 tablespoons of olive oil, 1 tablespoon of red wine vinegar, 1 crushed garlic clove and 1 teaspoon of mustard. Add a side of garlic bread and you'll be high-fiving yourself.

You can also make a big batch of this and freeze portions to eat later in the week.

BANGING SAUCY MEATBALLS

Serves 3–4

Meatballs are meant to make us happy, it's as simple as that, but not all meatballs are created equal. These meatballs are somewhat crazy, delicious, adventurous and a touch spicy all rolled into one. The sauce is easy to make and can also be used as a pizza sauce. Alright, enough of the chit-chat – let's get going.

WHAT YOU'LL NEED

large handful of plain potato chips

250 g pork mince

250 g beef mince

½ onion, finely chopped

3 garlic cloves, finely chopped

15 g (½ cup) basil leaves, finely chopped, plus whole basil leaves to serve

1 egg

1 tablespoon smoked paprika

1 teaspoon chilli powder

1 teaspoon salt flakes

1 teaspoon freshly ground black pepper

2 tablespoons plain flour

1 tablespoon olive oil

crusty bread, to serve

SAUCY TOMATO SAUCE

2 x 400 g cans diced tomatoes (splash out and get the Italian ones)

2 garlic cloves, finely chopped

1 tablespoon olive oil

1 teaspoon sugar

1 teaspoon salt flakes

½ teaspoon freshly ground black pepper

LET'S DO THIS!

We're going to start with the sauce – it's so easy! Place all the ingredients in a saucepan over medium heat. Give them a stir, then drop the heat so the sauce simmers but doesn't boil. Now step aside and enjoy the delicious smell. Cook over low heat for 25 minutes, by which time the sauce will have reduced and thickened, which is just how we want it.

Meanwhile, to make the banging meatballs, you'll need a mixing bowl, so stop reading and grab the bowl. Sorry, I forgot to mention, please also grab a zip-lock bag. Now put the potato chips in the zip-lock bag and lightly crush them with your fingers, until they're broken up into different sizes. There's no need to grab a rolling pin or pulverise them against the wall.

Drop both types of mince into the bowl, followed by the onion, garlic and basil. Crack in the egg, then add the crushed potato chips and all the remaining ingredients except the bread. Roll up your sleeves and start mixing with your hands, squishing the mixture in your palms until it's a little sticky and the ingredients are well combined. Using wet hands, roll into twelve golf ball–sized meatballs. Line the base of your air fryer with baking paper, then pop the meatballs in and cook on 175°C for 15 minutes, turning them every 5 minutes so they are evenly caramelised.

Transfer the meatballs to a shallow serving bowl and pour the delicious tomato sauce all over the top. Finish with some extra basil leaves and serve with crusty bread for mopping up the sauce.

 EXTRA FANCY STUFF The meatballs and sauce can be added to any pasta or even rice to turn them into a complete family meal. If you're feeling fancy, slice a baguette into 1 cm thick slices and top with a meatball and some sauce for the perfect finger food.

THAI-STYLE SATAY CHICKEN

Serves 4

Satay chicken was my first introduction to Thai food and I've been a big lover of the cuisine ever since. This recipe combines tricks I learned at a Thai cooking class in Phuket, as well as influences from my local Thai restaurant. It's also both easy and delicious.

STUFF TO GET

6 chicken thigh fillets

2 tablespoons peanut oil

1 teaspoon salt flakes

1 teaspoon freshly ground black pepper

400 ml can coconut cream

1 tablespoon Thai green curry paste

60 g (¼ cup) smooth peanut butter

1 teaspoon brown sugar

1 onion, finely chopped

2 garlic cloves, crushed

1 red capsicum, sliced into strips

3 spring onions, cut into 3–4 cm lengths, plus extra, sliced diagonally, to serve

TO SERVE

steamed rice

25 g (¼ cup) bean sprouts

1 long red chilli, finely sliced

40 g (¼ cup) chopped unsalted peanuts

3 coriander sprigs, leaves picked

LET'S ROCK IT LIKE THIS

First, we need to brown the chicken thighs and give them a good sear to make the skin crispy and golden. Pop them in a baking dish that will fit in your air fryer, drizzle over the peanut oil and season with the salt and pepper. Crank the air fryer to 220°C and cook for 6 minutes.

Meanwhile, grab a bowl and add the coconut cream, remembering to shake the can first as the coconut water usually separates from the cream. Add 100 ml of water, the curry paste, peanut butter, brown sugar, onion, garlic, capsicum and spring onion and give everything a good mix.

Pour the sauce all over the chicken, then reduce the air fryer temperature to 170°C and cook for 17 minutes or until the chicken is cooked through.

Is it ready yet? Good! Now to serve, I like to use small bowls and serve the rice separately for visual effect. Place the chicken thighs in the bowls and spoon the sauce all over the top. For the finishing touches, top with the bean sprouts, chilli, chopped peanuts, coriander leaves and extra spring onion. This recipe has the potential for 1000 Instagram likes, so share it and be proud.

OTHER COOL STUFF

If you are vegetarian or vegan, all you have to do is swap the chicken for chopped eggplant and potato. How easy is that?

Satay beef is also popular. If you'd like to try this, cut three porterhouse steaks into 5 mm thick slices and cook in the sauce (don't sear the beef, otherwise it will be tough).

SMOKIN' FISH TACOS

Makes 6

The last time I made fish tacos it took me ages to clean the fish tank and the fish didn't even eat the tacos! Sorry, not sorry – Dad joke. I know you're probably still laughing, but do try to read on. These tacos are light, tangy and so damn good! The simple chilli mayo is a game changer so, without further delay, here we go.

YOU'LL NEED ALL THIS

1 teaspoon plain flour

1 tablespoon smoked paprika

1 teaspoon salt flakes

1 teaspoon freshly ground
black pepper, plus extra to serve

250 g skinless, boneless barramundi
fillets, finely sliced (you should end
up with about 12–16 strips)

125 g (½ cup) mayonnaise

2 tablespoons sriracha chilli sauce

1 avocado

1 teaspoon olive oil

6 small, soft flour tortillas

coriander leaves, to serve

lime wedges, to serve

THIS IS HOW WE DO IT

Grab a small bowl, add the flour, paprika, salt and pepper and give it a good mix with a fork. Season the barramundi with this magic mixture by either sprinkling it over the fish or by dunking the fish into the bowl and covering it entirely. Set aside until the fish absorbs the seasoning mixture. The mixture will draw out moisture from the fish, which is a good thing.

Line the base of your air fryer with baking paper and add the fish in a single layer. Cook on 170°C for 12 minutes. Check the fish at the halfway mark to ensure it's not burning; if it's looking a little too crispy, reduce the heat to 155°C.

Meanwhile, combine the mayonnaise and sriracha chilli sauce in a small bowl or jar and set aside. Scoop the avocado into another bowl, add the olive oil and mash it up with a fork until it looks nice and silky.

Transfer the fish to a plate and drop the tortillas into the air fryer. Increase the heat to 200°C and warm the tortillas for 2 minutes or so.

To build your fish tacos, spread a tablespoon of mashed avocado over each tortilla and place two or three pieces of fish on top. Drizzle with as much of the chilli mayonnaise as you like, scatter over a little or a lot of coriander and top with some black pepper. Serve with lime wedges.

MORE THINGS

I like to use barramundi in my tacos, but feel free to go for any fish you like – you can even use chicken if you want, but, for me, there's nothing like barramundi with chilli mayo and lime juice.

If you are one of those people who say coriander tastes like soap, please call a helpline or shoot me an email, we need to talk.

I like to use sriracha chilli sauce, but you can use any chilli sauce. If you are not a chilli person, just add ½ teaspoon of tomato sauce. It's okay, I won't hold it against you.

EASY TERIYAKI-GLAZED SALMON SALAD

Serves 4

When I first learned how to make teriyaki sauce, I served it with everything. I made teriyaki chicken, teriyaki pork, teriyaki beef and this teriyaki salmon salad. This is such a funky, versatile recipe that you will even want to serve teriyaki sauce on your teriyaki sauce!

YOU WILL NEED

4 x 200 g boneless salmon fillets, skin on

2 baby cos lettuces, halved lengthways and leaves separated

250 g cherry tomatoes, halved

½ Lebanese cucumber, halved lengthways, deseeded and sliced

½ red onion, finely sliced

2 tablespoons extra-virgin olive oil

1 teaspoon lemon juice

sliced spring onion, to serve (optional)

TERIYAKI SAUCE

2½ tablespoons salt-reduced soy sauce

1½ tablespoons sweet sherry

1 tablespoon brown sugar

3 cm piece of ginger, finely grated

1 teaspoon maple syrup

ARE YOU READY?

To make the teriyaki sauce, combine the ingredients in a small bowl and stir until the sugar is dissolved.

Place the salmon in a shallow dish and pour the teriyaki sauce over the top, making sure the salmon is evenly coated. The secret here is to let the salmon rest and absorb the deliciousness of the sauce. So, cover the salmon with plastic wrap and put it in the fridge for about 1 hour.

Allow the salmon to come to room temperature. Line the base of your air fryer with baking paper and place the salmon on top (this will allow it to continue absorbing the marinade while it cooks, and the maple syrup and sugar in the sauce will caramelise beautifully). Cook on 165°C for 10 minutes or until the salmon is cooked through.

While the salmon cooks, combine the lettuce, tomato, cucumber and onion in a salad bowl. Drizzle over the olive oil and lemon juice and toss it all together.

Rest the salmon for 5 minutes, then cut it into whatever size you like, remembering that you want to keep as much of the glaze on the salmon as possible. Perch the salmon on top of the salad and top with some sliced spring onion, if you like. Grab a fork and don't even Instagram it, just start eating.

BONUS AWESOMENESS

You can also serve the teriyaki salmon on a bed of fluffy steamed rice. Delicious!

'COS I'M FREE' ROAST CAULIFLOWER AND VEGETABLE KEBABS

Serves 4

We all love a good Sunday roast, but it's usually reserved for meat-loving carnivores, right? Wrong! These days, vegetarians and vegans are also getting in on the action and this roasted cauliflower is an easy, delicious way to do it. My best friend Waz, who is vegan, loves me for it. When I was chatting to him recently he said to me, 'Bro, I think we should call the recipe "Cos I'm free" because it's free from anything that had a mother.' So here it is – enjoy!

WHAT YOU'LL NEED

2 tablespoons salt flakes

1 x 1 kg head of cauliflower

2 tablespoons olive oil

BASTING SAUCE

250 ml (1 cup) vegetable stock

1 tablespoon tomato paste

3 garlic cloves, crushed

1 tablespoon smoked paprika

1 tablespoon cornflour

1 teaspoon celery salt

VEGETABLE KEBABS

10 cherry tomatoes

1 red capsicum, cut into 2 cm pieces

1 red onion, cut into 8 wedges

200 g button mushrooms

1 zucchini, cut into 2 cm thick rounds

1 tablespoon olive oil

1 teaspoon salt flakes

LET'S MAKE MAGIC

Soak four bamboo or wooden skewers in water for 20 minutes.

Meanwhile, put a large saucepan of water on to boil and add half the salt. Remove any green leaves from the cauliflower and trim the base to make it flat, then pop the whole thing in the water and boil for 8 minutes.

To make the basting sauce, place all the ingredients in a small bowl and whisk until you have a thick sauce. Taste and adjust the seasonings, if you like.

Drain the cauliflower and sit it on a wire rack to cool and dry out a little. There will be a heap of steam coming from the cauliflower so be careful.

Let's make the kebabs. Start threading the veggies onto the skewers any which way you like – I often put a cherry tomato on each end so they keep everything together. Once complete, drizzle with the olive oil and sprinkle over the salt.

Use a pastry brush to brush the olive oil over the cauli, then sprinkle the remaining salt flakes on top. Line the base of your air fryer with baking paper and place the cauliflower in the middle. Arrange the kebabs around the cauli and cook on 180°C for 15 minutes, generously basting the cauli with the sauce every 3 minutes.

Transfer the cauliflower and kebabs to a serving dish and enjoy an awesome vegan Sunday roast that is quick enough to make any day of the week.

EXTRA, EXTRA, READ ALL ABOUT IT!

Did you know that cauliflower is extremely good for you? It's packed full of vitamin C and antioxidants that strengthen our immune systems. How good is that?

REAL-DEAL LASAGNE

Serves 4

When I was in Italy recently I discovered just how simple authentic lasagne should be. The produce was always the hero and there were no over-the-top ingredients. I figured the best way to make a lasagne in the air fryer was to take the same approach. This is a rich, meaty lasagne without white sauce, which, quite frankly, it doesn't need. When it comes to pasta sheets, I like to make my own, but you can use dried lasagne sheets if you don't have time.

GO GRAB THIS STUFF

2 tablespoons olive oil, plus extra for drizzling

250 g beef mince

250 g pork mince

1 onion, finely chopped

3 garlic cloves, crushed

1 tablespoon salt flakes, plus extra to serve

1 tablespoon freshly ground black pepper, plus extra to serve

2 x 400 g cans crushed tomatoes

1 bunch of basil, leaves picked

2 bay leaves

2 balls of buffalo mozzarella, roughly torn

50 g (½ cup) grated parmesan

Tomato and Garlic Focaccia (see page 48), to serve (optional)

LASAGNE SHEETS

300 g (2 cups) plain flour, plus extra for dusting

3 eggs

1 teaspoon salt flakes

LET'S MAKE THE LASAGNE SHEETS (SKIP TO THE SECOND PARAGRAPH IF USING DRIED SHEETS)

My rule of thumb for making pasta is 100 g of flour and one egg per person. So, get out your food processor, add the flour, eggs and salt and blitz until it forms a giant ball. Remove the dough and place it on a floured work surface. Knead really well for 10 minutes or until silky smooth. Cover with plastic wrap and rest in the fridge for 1 hour. Use a pasta machine or rolling pin to roll the dough out to 2 mm thick. Before you cut your lasagne sheets, choose four 500 ml (2 cup) capacity ramekins or tins to bake the lasagne in. Cut the pasta into sheets that will fit nicely in your ramekins or tins, then cover the pasta and set aside.

Place the olive oil, beef and pork mince, onion, garlic, salt and pepper in a baking dish that will fit in your air fryer. Stir well, then place in the air fryer and cook on 175°C for 3 minutes. Add the tomatoes, a small handful of the basil leaves and the bay leaves and cook for another 3 minutes. Empty the sauce into a bowl and let's get ready to assemble.

Drizzle your ramekins or tins with olive oil, add a layer of lasagne sheets, then spoon on enough sauce to cover the pasta. Top with some mozzarella, 1 tablespoon of the parmesan and a few basil leaves. Repeat until you either reach the top of the ramekins or tins or you run out of ingredients, but make sure you finish with a layer of cheese.

Cover with foil and cook on 180°C for 20 minutes. Remove the foil and cook for another 3 minutes. Top with basil leaves and some salt and pepper. Serve with my focaccia, if you like.

COOL TIPS Lasagne is like pizza in terms of preferences – some people include carrot or celery, others like a white sauce; heck, some even use chicken mince. There is no right or wrong way, there's only your way. I hope this recipe serves as a guide for you to make your own. However, if I discover that anyone has added pineapple to this recipe, I will find you!

SOUL PEPPERS

Makes 6

Soul peppers sounds like the name of a soul band, but they were actually my comfort food when I was a kid. It's crazy how I didn't appreciate the amazing food my mum made when I was little, yet here I am recreating her dishes. I recently started taking these soul peppers to work in a thermos. The smell in the office meant I had to write the recipe down several times.

GET THE FOLLOWING DELIVERED

1 tablespoon olive oil

200 g pork mince

1 onion, finely chopped

2 garlic cloves, finely chopped

1 tablespoon salt flakes

100 g (½ cup) long-grain white rice

1 teaspoon smoked paprika

1 teaspoon dried mint

6 red capsicums

2 large tomatoes, cut into 1 cm thick slices

freshly ground black pepper, to serve

chopped oregano leaves, to serve (optional)

THIS IS HOW WE DO IT

Place the olive oil, mince, onion, garlic, salt and 125 ml (½ cup) of water in a baking dish that will fit in your air fryer and give it a good stir. Cook on 175°C for 5 minutes. Add the rice, smoked paprika, dried mint and another 125 ml (½ cup) of water and cook for another 5 minutes.

Meanwhile, cut the tops off the capsicums and scoop out the seeds, but don't pierce the skin as they're going to house our filling. Using a soup spoon, fill the capsicums with the mince mixture, then place a slice of tomato on top to make a little lid.

Place the stuffed capsicums in the baking dish and pour 500 ml (2 cups) of water into the dish. Transfer to the air fryer, increase the heat to 190°C and cook for 15 minutes. The smell will be absolutely mind-blowing.

Pop the soul peppers on plates, drizzle over a little of the remaining liquid from the baking dish and top with some pepper and oregano, if you like. Enjoy.

 OTHER COOL STUFF **I remember my mum also sometimes added strips of bacon or salami, so feel free to use other ingredients that rock your world. You can swap out the pork mince for beef, chicken or even turkey mince if you like.**

CHICKEN PARMA NAPOLITANA

Serves 4

Is there anything better than a couple of beers or wines and a chicken parma at your local pub? Yes, I know there are better things, like a million dollars, but you know what I mean. Being able to make a classic dish in the air fryer in a fraction of the time with less clean up is what I call genius.

YOU WILL NEED

bread crusts from 4 slices of bread

3 tablespoons flat-leaf parsley leaves

1 teaspoon salt flakes

1 teaspoon garlic powder

3 tablespoons grated parmesan

150 g (1 cup) plain flour

2 eggs, lightly beaten

2 chicken breasts

olive oil spray

400 g can crushed tomatoes

4 slices of thick-cut deli ham

1 ball of buffalo mozzarella, roughly torn

basil leaves, to serve

green salad, to serve

Daddy's Famous Chips (see page 77), to serve (optional)

ARE YOU READY?

Blitz the bread crusts, parsley, salt, garlic powder and parmesan in a blender until you have a mixture of fine and coarse breadcrumbs. Transfer to a plate and set aside. Place the flour and beaten egg in separate shallow bowls.

Cut the chicken breasts in half horizontally, so you have four thinner pieces of chicken. Working with one piece at a time, cover the chicken with baking paper and use a meat mallet to bash it up real good, until it's half as thick again.

Dredge the chicken in the flour, then dip into the beaten egg and then straight into the breadcrumb mixture to completely coat. Did you get that? Flour, egg, breadcrumbs.

Place the breaded chicken on a baking tray that will fit in your air fryer (you may need to do two batches) and give it a light spray with olive oil. Cook on 180°C for 7 minutes, then remove the tray from the air fryer. Flip the chicken over and spread 2 tablespoons of the crushed tomatoes over each fillet, then top with a slice of ham and another 2 tablespoons of tomato sauce. Finally, scatter over the mozzarella, just like a pizza. Now pop the tray back in the air fryer and cook for another 7 minutes until the chicken is golden and the cheese is melted.

Transfer your parmas to plates, scatter a few basil leaves over and serve with a green salad and my chips, if you like.

OTHER COOL STUFF

If you want to mix things up, you can use pork or beef fillets, but it won't be called a chicken parma, LOL. You can also swap the mozzarella for another cheese, such as gruyere, and use bacon instead of ham, or omit it entirely.

'YOU'RE WELCOME' ROAST POTATOES

Serves 4 as a side

I have made many attempts to cook the perfect roast potatoes. I have hopped on one foot while watching them cook, and stared into the oven while praying to the roast potato gods, but to no avail. That is until I developed this ridiculously tasty recipe. I have roasted all varieties of potato in my time, so trust me when I tell you this: buy Dutch cream potatoes. End of story.

STUFF TO GET

2 tablespoons salt flakes

8 Dutch cream potatoes, peeled and quartered

1 tablespoon olive oil

6–8 garlic cloves, peeled

3 tablespoons duck fat

2 rosemary sprigs, leaves picked, plus extra to serve (optional)

ARE YOU READY?

There are two components to making awesome roast potatoes. First, we are going to parboil the potatoes. Bring a large saucepan of water to the boil and stir through half the salt. Add the potato, then reduce the heat to medium and cook for 8 minutes.

Drain, then transfer the potato to a roasting tin that will fit in your air fryer. Use a fork to pierce and score the spuds so they're a little rough round the edges. Add the olive oil and throw in the garlic.

Microwave the duck fat until it turns to liquid – this usually takes 40 seconds on high. Pour the duck fat over the potato, then sprinkle over the remaining salt and the rosemary and toss well to coat.

Pop the potatoes in your air fryer to cook on 180°C for 15–17 minutes and wait for a beautiful smell to hit the kitchen. About halfway through, check on the spuds: if they're golden brown, turn them over, but be gentle as they will be fragile. Continue to cook until completely golden.

Top with some extra rosemary, if you like, and serve the roast potatoes as a delicious side, with or without the garlic cloves.

ALSO TRY THIS!

Remember the pork crackling lettuce cups on page 62? Serve these roast potatoes with the pork belly and you have a match made in roast-dinner heaven.

If you see someone dip these spuds in tomato sauce, please call the police.

If you are not a fan of duck fat, add an extra tablespoon of olive oil instead to make an amazing vegan side dish.

YORKSHIRE PUDDINGS

Makes 6

I didn't grow up in the UK and my Macedonian upbringing didn't allow for Yorkshire puddings, so this is a new dish for me and my family, but I tell you what, they're so good and easy to make. What I love about this recipe is that my British friends say it reminds them of their childhood. So rush into the kitchen and let's get cracking.

YOU WILL NEED

2 eggs

100 ml milk

100 g (⅔ cup) plain flour

125 ml (½ cup) sunflower oil

ARE YOU READY?

Firstly, preheat the air fryer on 190°C for 5 minutes. Let's get that game changer hot and ready.

I like to use a protein shaker to mix my ingredients, so crack it open and in this order add the eggs, milk and flour. Shake it for 3 minutes, almost like you're having a three-year-old tantrum. We want the ingredients to mix and blend really well. Don't laugh, just keep shaking.

Grab six 8 cm diameter ramekins and evenly divide the sunflower oil among them. Pop the ramekins in the air fryer and leave them to heat up for 5 minutes.

Working very carefully as the oil will be hot, evenly pour the batter into each ramekin, stopping about 5 mm from the top (the batter will start sizzling but don't stress as this is normal). Reduce the air fryer temperature to 180°C and cook for 12 minutes or until your Yorkshire puddings rise and shine.

Now you can put on three jumpers, a scarf, gloves and a beanie and pretend you're from the UK.

 EXTRA FUN STUFF Traditionally, Yorkshire puddings are eaten with a roast and you pour gravy all over them. However, I find they're so versatile that you can turn them into a delicious sweet treat. Fill them with jam or chocolate–hazelnut spread and dust some icing sugar over the top – they taste just like eclairs. Just don't tell a British person that it took an Aussie to figure this out!

Muffins, cakes, cookies, pastries and desserts – all the good stuff, no fuss

SWEETS
THAT MAKE YOU GO
MMM...

BANANA BREAKFAST HEAVEN

Serves 4

Breakfast can be a tricky task, but what if I said this recipe will have your kids eating fresh fruit, natural yoghurt and cereal for breakfast and absolutely loving it? Don't believe me? Continue reading below.

YOU'LL NEED ALL THIS...

60 g (2 cups) cornflakes

2½ tablespoons melted butter

2½ tablespoons honey, plus extra for drizzling

4 bananas

500 g (2 cups) natural yoghurt

NOW WHAT?

Put the cornflakes in a large zip-lock bag, zip it tight and beat the crap out of them, making sure you don't burst the bag (placing the bag under a tea towel will help here). You want the cornflakes to be different sizes (some can be crumbs while others can be about 1 cm – it doesn't matter too much).

Now pour the butter and honey into the zip-lock bag and mix it a little so it's evenly distributed. Add the bananas and use your fingers to massage the cornflake mixture all over the bananas.

Line the base of your air fryer with baking paper (or use a non-stick baking dish). Tip the cornflake-coated bananas onto the paper or into the dish and cook in the air fryer on 170°C for 8 minutes. The bananas will look lovely and golden.

Divide among plates and dollop the yoghurt on the side. Sprinkle any remaining cornflake crumbs from the zip-lock bag over top and drizzle with some extra honey, if you like.

You can make this recipe with other fruit, such as pineapple. Basically, it's a healthy fruit fritter without the deep-frying, hence the reason air fryers are the best thing ever.*

*Conditions apply, Pearl Jam is the best thing ever.

HOT JAM MUFFINS

Makes 6

I think this recipe is borderline genius (or crazy). When I first made these jam muffins my wife stood there watching me saying, 'How the hell does your mind come up with this stuff?'. When I posted the video on Instagram it went ballistic – 3.5 million hits in less than a week. So dig out what you need and let's get cracking.

GRAB THE FOLLOWING

1 egg

250 ml (1 cup) milk

3 tablespoons melted butter

3 tablespoons maple syrup

150 g (1 cup) self-raising flour

olive oil spray or butter

1 kids' medicine syringe (trust me)

1½ tablespoons raspberry jam

1 tablespoon icing sugar, sifted

raspberries, to serve (optional)

mint leaves, to serve (optional)

WHAT'S NEXT?

First up, grab your protein shaker or use a mixing bowl and whisk. Add the egg, milk, melted butter, maple syrup and flour. Either shake the ingredients like there's no tomorrow or whisk them really well.

Grab a six-hole muffin tin that will fit in your air fryer or use six 8 cm diameter ramekins. If your muffin tin is non-stick, bonus; otherwise, grease the holes with olive oil spray or butter. Divide the muffin mixture evenly among the muffin holes or ramekins but only fill them two-thirds of the way up, as the mixture will rise.

Pop the tin or ramekins in your air fryer and cook on 170°C for 7 minutes. They will rise up and may even overflow, but that's okay as you'll have more to eat.

While the muffins are cooling down, grab the syringe and, using kitchen scissors, snip the top off so you have a bigger hole. Put the syringe in the jam and suck it up – you should have about 5 ml of jam. This next bit is the best: insert the syringe into the centre of a muffin and push in the jam (I know, genius, right?). Once you have filled all the muffins, dust the icing sugar over the top.

You can serve these as is, or scatter over some fresh raspberries and mint leaves if you want to impress people. Enjoy moderately (just kidding, these are not deep-fried, so eat them all if you want).

I have made these with strawberry jam, too, and they were delicious, so use any flavour you like. Or for a complete game changer, you could use chocolate–hazelnut spread and be the first human ever to make air-fried hot chocolate–hazelnut muffins. OMG!

MINI CROISSANTS

Makes 32

Don't think big when it comes to school lunches, think small. Kids don't want to sit down and eat a massive croissant at lunchtime, they want to play with their friends and cause havoc. So I had an idea to create bite-sized croissants instead. Let's face it, this isn't a recipe as such, it's just an awesome idea that you need to be a little crafty with – so let's get crafty.

WHAT YOU'LL NEED

2 sheets of frozen puff pastry, just thawed

1 egg, lightly beaten

strawberry yoghurt, to serve (optional)

WHAT'S NEXT?

Cut one pastry sheet in half and then in half again so that you have four long strips of pastry. Lay the pastry strips horizontally in front of you and cut each strip into four squares. Now cut each square diagonally in half to make a triangle. You should end up with a total of 32 triangles.

Grab your second sheet of puff pastry and do the same, except cut each long pastry strip into six pieces instead of four. Then cut each piece diagonally in half to make triangles. Keep cutting until you have 32 smaller triangles. You won't need the whole pastry sheet, so roll the leftover pastry into a ball, cover with plastic wrap and return to the freezer to use another day.

Okay, so now you have two different-sized triangles. Place a small triangle on top of a large triangle (aligned at the base) and lightly press. Flip it over and roll it up from the base like a French pastry chef in Paris. Pop your mini croissant on a baking tray that will fit in your air fryer, then repeat with the remaining triangles. Grab your pastry brush thingy and brush the croissants with the beaten egg.

Pop the mini croissants in the air fryer in batches and cook on 175°C for 12 minutes. When they're ready, you will eat at least half of them. Put the other half in your kids' lunchboxes, or serve with some strawberry yoghurt to dip into, if you like.

EXTRA FUN STUFF

Some people ask me why I don't put anything inside the mini croissants. My kids like to eat them plain, but feel free to add whatever you like before rolling them up: a little cheese and ham will make a savoury croissant, or add a square of dark chocolate and a few mini marshmallows for a sweet treat. Either way, make it your own and have fun with them as the ultimate plan is for your little human to actually eat something during school lunchtime.

DEDO'S GEVREK

Makes 16

'What on earth is Dedo's gevrek?' I hear you ask. Okay, so here's the story. My grandfather was a baker back in Macedonia and whenever we went to visit him and the rest of my family, he would bring me a gevrek from his bakery. It's like a New York–style pretzel covered in sesame seeds and cooked with honey. My mum only recently found the original recipe in my grandfather's handwriting. These gevrek are so dear to me, and I really hope you enjoy them.

YOU WILL NEED

2 x 7 g sachets dried yeast

pinch of sugar

500 ml (2 cups) lukewarm water

pinch of salt flakes

800 g plain flour, plus extra for dusting

3 tablespoons honey

155 g (1 cup) sesame seeds

natural yoghurt, to serve (optional)

LET'S MAKE MAGIC

Combine the yeast, sugar and water in a large bowl and set aside for about 15 minutes, until it looks all frothy. Add the salt and flour and mix really well with a fork. Once it gets too thick, tip onto a floured work surface, swap the fork for your hands and knead for about 10 minutes, until you have a smooth dough. Place the dough in a lightly oiled bowl, cover with plastic wrap and leave on the bench to do its thing for 40 minutes. It will rise beautifully.

Line a large baking tray with baking paper.

Return the dough to your work surface and knead again for about 3 minutes. Divide the dough into sixteen even-sized portions. Roll the portions into 25 cm long logs, then join the ends of each log to create a ring. Pop the dough rings on the prepared tray.

Combine the honey and 1 litre (4 cups) of water in a saucepan over medium heat and whisk until the honey has dissolved. Bring to the boil, then, working in batches of four, lower the dough rings into the sweetened water and cook for 3 minutes.

Meanwhile, spread the sesame seeds on a large plate. Using tongs, remove the dough rings from the water and dip them, one by one, into the sesame seeds until they are completely covered. Set aside to rest for 10 minutes.

Line the base of your air fryer with baking paper and cook the dough rings, four at a time, on 180°C for 15 minutes. They should turn a beautiful golden brown and smell divine.

Allow the gevrek to cool a little, then enjoy them while they're still warm. As a kid, I remember eating these with natural yoghurt, but they are equally good on their own.

EXTRA FANCY STUFF These gevrek are only slightly sweet, but if you want to ramp up the sweetness, simply drizzle them with an extra tablespoon of honey when you take them out of the air fryer.

AUTUMN LEAVES APPLE PIE DELIGHT

Serves 8

This recipe is inspired by a red apple I once saw sitting among autumn leaves on the forest floor next to some rare white truffles. Okay, not really, but it does sound like the coolest introduction to a recipe. If you really want to know, I was originally going to make this a cheese and onion pie, but onions make my girls fart big time, so I decided to make an apple pie delight instead. Now THAT'S the best recipe intro ever.

GO GRAB THIS STUFF

6 sheets of filo pastry

3 tablespoons melted butter

4 pink lady apples, cored, halved and cut into 2 mm thick slices

2 tablespoons sugar

1 teaspoon ground cinnamon

maple syrup, to serve (optional)

vanilla ice cream, to serve

NOW DO THIS

If you've got one of those fancy round pie tins, then great; otherwise, use a regular round baking dish. Either way, it needs to be 25 cm in diameter, so find a ruler and measure up. If your pastry is frozen, allow it to thaw out for 30 minutes; if it's refrigerated, just take it out of the fridge 10 minutes before you want to start.

Brush the base and side of your pie tin or baking dish with 1 tablespoon of the butter.

Cut the filo into 5 cm wide strips (you need 20–25 strips). Working with one strip at a time, lay the strip horizontally in front of you and start placing the sliced apples along the top half of the strip with the rounded edge of the apple slices facing away from you and overlapping them by 5 mm. Fold the bottom edge of the filo strip over the apple slices, then roll it up onto itself and pop it in the centre of the tin or dish, with the apple facing upwards. Repeat with the remaining filo strips and apple slices, but instead of rolling up the pastry, wrap it around the central apple roll in the tin or dish. Keep working outwards until you can't fit any more in. You should now be looking at a giant snail of apple delight.

This is the cool bit now – with a pastry brush, gently brush the remaining melted butter all over the top. Mix the sugar and cinnamon in a small bowl and sprinkle it all over the pie. If you like, you can pre-slice the uncooked pie so it's easier to cut once cooked. Pop it in the air fryer to cook on 170°C for 12 minutes and wait for a delicious smell to fill the kitchen.

Drizzle with a little maple syrup, if you like, and serve with some vanilla ice cream.

 COOL TIPS **If you are thinking of using other fruit, feel free to experiment with sliced pears or strawberries, but please don't use citrus fruits.**

SUPER SPEEDY HONEY JOYS

Makes 12

I love using flat-bottom ice cream cones. They save on patty-pan cases, which are just thrown out anyway, so think of this recipe as doing your bit for the environment by eating. How cool is that? I don't know anyone who didn't eat honey joys as a kid. This simple recipe is a party favourite with a twist.

2½ tablespoons butter

55 g (¼ cup) caster sugar

1 tablespoon maple syrup or honey

60 g (2 cups) cornflakes

12 flat-bottom ice cream cones

1 tablespoon icing sugar, sifted

THIS IS HOW WE DO IT

Place the butter, sugar and maple syrup or honey in a small saucepan over medium heat. Stir the mixture until it starts to froth and bubble, then remove from the heat. Add the cornflakes and stir until they are completely coated in the sugary, buttery mixture.

Using a spoon, fill the ice cream cones with the cornflake mixture until they're overly full – the higher the better (remember, they need to look awesome). Once you've done this, and secretly eaten a few tablespoons of the mixture, sit them upright in the air fryer and cook on 150°C for 6 minutes. The smell of the butter and maple syrup or honey will be truly amazing.

Remove from the air fryer, lightly dust with icing sugar and serve. Don't worry about storage instructions as they'll be gone before you know it.

OTHER COOL STUFF You can leave out the icing sugar, but it does make the honey joys look even more spectacular. You can use healthier cereal options, but I figure if you are going to make honey joys you might as well eat them as nature intended; however, do eat them in moderation (said no one ever).

GIANT M&M'S COOKIE

Makes 1 giant cookie

This cookie is inspired by my sister, Suzy, who tries to limit herself to one biscuit at a time, but then complains that they're never big enough. So, I decided to invent a giant M&M's cookie in her honour. It is a game changer that looks amazing and tastes great, but, most importantly, rocks any kid's birthday party.

YOU'LL NEED ALL THIS

125 g softened butter

125 g (⅔ cup) brown sugar

3 tablespoons golden syrup

1 egg

225 g (1½ cups) self-raising flour

200 g M&M's

THIS IS HOW WE DO IT

Using a stand mixer with a whisk or electric beaters, cream together the butter and sugar for 1 minute. Add the golden syrup and egg. Watch it go round and round for another minute, then add the flour and let the mixer do its thing for another 2 minutes.

Spoon the cookie mixture onto baking paper and spread it out to a 30 cm circle, about 1 cm thick.

Now for the fun part. Decorate the cookie with the M&M's. Use all the colours and make sure it looks super fun. Pop it in the air fryer and cook on 175°C for 8 minutes.

If you have leftover cookie dough, cook a batch of smaller cookies; that way you can Instagram them with the giant one as a size comparison – guaranteed likes right there.

 M&M's are my chocolate of choice, but you can go crazy with different options. Imagine using Maltesers or even crushed KitKat or Crunchie. Alternatively, keep it simple and just use choc chips. #legend

GAME-CHANGER BAKLAVA

Serves only me (or 8)

When I told my mum that I was making baklava in my air fryer she said, 'I don't believe it', but in her cute Macedonian accent. I was surprised at how easy it is to make, which kind of upset me as I've missed out on years of baklava because I thought it was too hard. My mum came over and we made this recipe together step by step and I took notes along the way. So here it is, just for you.

GET THE FOLLOWING DELIVERED

200 g (2 cups) walnuts

50 g (⅓ cup) shelled unsalted pistachio nuts

125 ml (½ cup) vegetable oil

60 g (½ cup) semolina

375 g packet of filo pastry (defrosted if frozen)

vanilla ice cream, to serve (optional)

SUGAR SYRUP

440 g (2 cups) sugar

finely grated zest and juice of ½ lemon

LET'S DO THIS!

Time to crush some nuts! I like to use my blender to blitz the walnuts, but if you don't have a blender, put the walnuts in a zip-lock bag and smash the crap out of them. Now do the same with your pistachios. Set the nuts aside and don't mix the walnuts with the pistachios, okay?

Let's make the sugar syrup. Place 1 litre (4 cups) of water, the sugar and lemon zest and juice in a saucepan over medium heat and give it a quick stir to combine the ingredients. Simmer for 30 minutes without stirring again – the liquid will reduce but don't freak out!

Now we are going to assemble the baklava. Brush the base and side of a round, loose-base tart tin with a little of the vegetable oil. Sprinkle over some semolina, then place three sheets of filo in the base (the pastry will hang over the edge of the tin, but chill, we'll fix that later). Brush with a little more vegetable oil, sprinkle over more semolina and top with 3 tablespoons of the crushed walnuts. Repeat this process until the pastry reaches the top of the tin, then finish with the pistachios. Use a rolling pin to press down around the edge of the tin and perfectly trim the overhanging pastry.

Pop the tin in the air fryer and cook on 180°C for 5 minutes, then reduce the temperature to 140°C and cook for another 15 minutes or until golden brown.

Remember this fact: the pastry needs to be cool before you pour over the syrup, otherwise it will go soggy. So let the baklava cool down – it should take about 1 hour – then pour the syrup over the top and let it sit for a few hours to soak in. Serve with ice cream, if you like, and enjoy this blissful recipe.

 OTHER COOL STUFF

Walnuts and pistachios are traditionally used in baklava, but I have also used macadamias and the baklava takes on a whole new buttery taste. So don't be afraid to try different combinations of nuts, or even lime or orange zest instead of lemon zest. Go nuts and make this recipe your own.

CHURROS CAKES

Makes 6

Yes, you read that correctly: churros cakes. I was recently experimenting with my air fryer and I thought I'd have a crack at making churros, but for some reason my instincts led me to put the mixture in ramekins. What happened next was a complete accident, but if making mistakes enables me to create recipes like this, then I think I'll make more mistakes in the future.

250 ml (1 cup) melted butter

2 tablespoons caster sugar

large pinch of salt flakes

6 eggs

300 g (2 cups) plain flour

CINNAMON–SUGAR TOPPING

2 tablespoons caster sugar

1 teaspoon ground cinnamon

CHOCOLATE–HAZELNUT TOPPING

2 tablespoons chocolate–hazelnut spread

1 tablespoon milk

SUGAR SYRUP TOPPING

80 ml (⅓ cup) sugar syrup (see page 135)

LET'S MAKE THIS!

Put the kettle on – no, not for a cuppa, you need 250 ml (1 cup) of boiling water. Pour the boiling water into a heatproof bowl and add the melted butter, sugar and salt. Using a fork, stir the mixture for 1 minute, then add an egg and stir again for another 30 seconds. Repeat this process with the remaining eggs, stirring for 30 seconds after each addition. Add the flour and stir until you have a warm, fluffy and sticky dough. Don't stress if you are wondering how you are going to knead it, as there's no kneading necessary.

Grab six 10 cm diameter ramekins and grease them with butter (I usually scrape out the bowl that had the melted butter). Divide the dough among the ramekins until they are three-quarters full.

Pop the ramekins in the air fryer and cook on 170°C for 15 minutes or until the cakes look golden and delicious.

While the cakes are cooking, prepare your toppings. Combine the sugar and cinnamon in a small bowl. Now put the chocolate–hazelnut spread and milk in a heatproof jug and zap it in the microwave for 20 seconds on high. Stir until the mixture is smooth and glossy.

Remove the churros cakes from the ramekins and place on a cooling rack or tray. Sprinkle two of the cakes with the cinnamon sugar, drizzle the chocolate–hazelnut topping over another two cakes and spoon the sugar syrup over the last two cakes. Now leave everyone to fight over who gets what!

EXTRA, EXTRA, READ ALL ABOUT IT!

Feel free to add different toppings depending on what mood you're in. I also like to use jam, ice cream, caramel sauce and lemon and sugar (but not all at once).

Traditional churros are deep-fried in oil, so this is a guilt-free alternative, meaning you can eat as many as you want.

STRAWBERRY TRIANGLE DELIGHTS

Makes 8

These strawberry triangles are so easy that I can make them from start to finish in less than 10 minutes – yep, you read that right. Remember to always have frozen puff pastry on hand in the freezer for when you crave one of these delights.

GO GRAB THIS STUFF

2 sheets of frozen puff pastry, just thawed

90 g (½ cup) diced strawberries, plus extra whole strawberries to serve (optional)

2 tablespoons maple syrup

whipped cream, to serve (optional)

LET'S GET CRACKING

Cut the puff pastry sheets into quarters to make eight squares. Divide the diced strawberries evenly among the pastry squares, then fold the pastry over the strawberries to make triangles. Easy so far? Using a fork, press down the open edges so the strawberries are securely enclosed. Using a knife, score the tops of the pastry triangles with two or three lines about 2–3 cm long.

Using a pastry brush (don't use your finger like I did), brush the tops of the triangles with the maple syrup. Make sure they're completely covered as this is the only sweetener we are adding (strawberries can become a little bitter when cooked, so it is important to balance this out).

Line the base of your air fryer with baking paper and pop the strawberry triangles in. Cook on 180°C for 8 minutes. Before you've even had a chance to wash up, they will be ready. If you like, you can serve these with extra strawberries and whipped cream, but they are also awesome on their own.

MORE THINGS Whip these up for a sweet Sunday brunch or weekday dessert. If you don't have strawberries, try other berries. I have also filled these triangles with apple and cinnamon and dusted with icing sugar for a special touch. Yes, they were amazing.

CHOCOLATE-HAZELNUT MUFFIN CONES

Makes 6

These muffin cones are the bomb, and what I love most is that you don't need a muffin tin. That's right, everything is edible with this recipe, except the air fryer – you don't want to be eating that. These are the ultimate kid (or even adult) hand-held deliciousness.

STUFF TO GET

250 ml (1 cup) milk

1 egg

2 tablespoons melted butter

150 g (1 cup) self-raising flour

1 tablespoon sugar

6 flat-bottom ice cream cones

1 kids' medicine syringe

3 tablespoons chocolate–hazelnut spread (or more if you're a rebel)

2 tablespoons icing sugar, sifted

WHAT'S NEXT?

I love using my protein shaker for this recipe, so crack the lid and add the milk, egg, butter, flour and sugar. Now shake it up so that the mixture looks like a thickshake – this will take about 2 minutes. If you don't have a protein shaker you can whisk the ingredients in a bowl.

Sit the ice cream cones upright on your work surface and pour in the muffin mixture until you get 2 cm from the top. Remember, these bad boys will rise and we don't want them to cause a mess. Pop the cones upright in the air fryer, turn the dial to 175°C and cook for 7 minutes.

Now comes the wow part. Grab the medicine syringe and, using kitchen scissors, snip the top off so you have a bigger hole. Put the syringe in the chocolate–hazelnut spread and suck it up – you should have about 5 ml of spread. Now stick the syringe into a muffin and inject the chocolate–hazelnut spread into the centre. If you're a rebel, repeat the process again; otherwise, move on to the next muffin cone.

Dust the icing sugar over the top of the cones and eat them.

BONUS AWESOMENESS

It's okay to add two, three or four lots of chocolate–hazelnut spread into the muffins, just don't tell anyone. If you don't want to use chocolate–hazelnut spread, you can melt some dark or white chocolate instead. Peace out.

SUZY'S PISTACHIO AND HONEY PAV

Serves 4

Suzy is my sister and she's one of the most fun people I know. When we used to walk to school she'd protect me from the ants (I was petrified of ants, okay?) and turn a blind eye when I ate my weekly ration of treats in a day (and even when I'd break into her stash, too). That's total love right there. I decided to name this recipe after Suzy, because I love her unconditionally and she always made this pav for us when there was an occasion to celebrate.

YOU'LL NEED ALL THIS

4 egg whites, at room temperature

pinch of salt flakes

200 g caster sugar

1 tablespoon cornflour

1 teaspoon white vinegar

300 ml double cream

3 tablespoons roughly chopped unsalted pistachios

1 teaspoon ground cinnamon

3 tablespoons runny honey

NOW WHAT?

Make sure the eggs are at room temperature. Why? Because that's what my sister said you have to do. I use a stand mixer thingy with the whisk attached to make this rockin' pav. Drop the egg whites and salt into the bowl and whisk on high until soft peaks form. Continue to whisk and slowly add the sugar, a tablespoon at a time, every 45 seconds (if you add the sugar all at once your meringue will be grainy). Once you've added all the sugar, the meringue should look white and glossy. Add the cornflour and vinegar and whisk for another 2–3 minutes.

Line the base of your air fryer with baking paper. Using a dessertspoon, scoop the meringue onto the baking paper and spread it out to form a 25 cm circle. Don't worry too much about being a perfectionist as we'll be topping the pav later on with delicious cream. Cook on 170°C for 3 minutes, then reduce the temperature to 140°C and cook for 40 minutes.

Very carefully remove the cooked meringue from the air fryer. You will be tempted to immediately add toppings, but you have to let it cool down completely. Once it is cool (and not a minute before), whip the cream to stiff peaks and get ready to channel your inner Da Vinci. Spoon the whipped cream onto the meringue, top with the pistachios and cinnamon and drizzle over the honey.

 If you're a play-it-safe type of person, you can go the traditional berry pavlova. Just grab a punnet of strawberries and half a punnet each of raspberries and blueberries. Spread them all over the whipped cream and dust with icing sugar.

THE '80s COMEBACK CAKE

Serves 6

Okay, it's time to tease up the hair and bring out the puffy shoulder pads. This upside-down pineapple cake is cooler than Duran Duran and Culture Club put together. My mum used to make pineapple cake for my sister and me in her Bessemer stovetop pan, and it was always the highlight of our week. My version takes a slightly more modern approach, cooking individual cakes in ramekins so that a) they fit in the air fryer and b) everyone gets a perfect round of pineapple.

STUFF TO GET

150 g softened butter

100 g brown sugar

½ teaspoon ground cinnamon

6 rings of canned pineapple in syrup, drained

180 g sugar

2 eggs

½ teaspoon vanilla extract

200 g (1⅓ cups) self-raising flour

130 g natural yoghurt

TIME TO STAND AND DELIVER THE FOLLOWING

Spread 50 g of the butter among the bases of six 7 cm diameter ramekins. Combine the brown sugar and cinnamon in a small bowl, then sprinkle the mixture over the butter and pop a pineapple ring on top so it sits nice and snug.

Back in the '80s, my mum used a hand-held mixer with the two whisks going 100 miles a second, but I like to use a stand mixer with the whisk attached. Place the remaining butter and the sugar in the bowl and mix until nice and fluffy. Add the eggs, vanilla and three-quarters of the flour and mix again for 30 seconds. Add the yoghurt and the remaining flour and mix for 1 minute.

Spoon the cake batter into the ramekins until they are about three-quarters full, then transfer to the air fryer and cook on 175°C for 17 minutes or until the cakes have risen and a skewer inserted into the middle of a cake comes out clean. Use this time to watch a little *Miami Vice* or tease your hair, but please don't forget the hairspray.

Allow the pineapple cakes to cool a little, then run a knife around the cakes, upend the ramekins and turn them out into shallow serving bowls.

 EXTRA FANCY STUFF

I remember some pineapple cakes in the '80s had a glacé cherry placed in the pineapple hole to give it extra bang, because back then more was better.

If you are not a fan of yoghurt you can use sour cream. Oh, and remember that this is a sweet cake because of the two types of sugar and the pineapple, so please eat in moderation. LOL, just kidding.

ESPRESSO-CUP FRIED BANANAS

Makes 9

I love this recipe for two reasons: first, fried bananas taste ridiculously good; and second (which is really my first reason), you can't share them. Amazing, right? I've always loved fried bananas, but there's something even more special about air-fried bananas. This dish is so simple you'll wonder why no one ever made them like this before.

YOU WILL NEED

1 sheet of frozen puff pastry, just thawed

3–4 tablespoons maple syrup

3 tablespoons softened butter

3 bananas, cut into 1 cm thick slices

3 tablespoons brown sugar

1 tablespoon icing sugar, sifted

LET'S MAKE MAGIC

First, we are going to make lids with the puff pastry. Cut the pastry sheet into nine squares and score the tops with diagonal lines. Transfer to a sheet of baking paper and drizzle with 1 tablespoon of the maple syrup. Lift up the baking paper and pop the pastry in the air fryer on 180°C for 7 minutes or until puffed up and golden.

While your pastry lids are cooking, grab nine espresso cups and distribute the butter evenly among them. Add the banana, then drizzle over the remaining maple syrup and sprinkle over the brown sugar.

Remove the pastry lids from the air fryer once they are cooked, then pop the banana espresso cups in. Cook on 180°C for 7 minutes (you might need to do this in batches). Once you hear the magic 'beep beep' coming from the air fryer, it's time to indulge. Top the espresso cups with the pastry squares, dust over the icing sugar and serve.

Does it need to be bananas? Not really, you can also try pineapple, strawberries or even apples. I like to be resourceful and use what I have on hand or what the neighbour has hanging over the fence. You can limit the sweetness by reducing or omitting the maple syrup or brown sugar.

Serving these with some vanilla ice cream is an excellent idea.

BERRY YOGHURT PIZZA

Serves 2

This recipe is the bomb and a guaranteed crowd-pleaser. Whenever I make something that looks remotely like pizza, the kids go nuts for it. A year or so ago I did an Instagram collaboration with a yoghurt company and they asked me to create a new recipe, and this was the result. The response was huge and, most importantly, I received positive feedback from parents with fussy kids. Here it is.

YOU'LL NEED ALL THIS

80 g strawberry yoghurt

35 g (¼ cup) sliced strawberries

40 g (¼ cup) blueberries

30 g (¼ cup) raspberries

3 tablespoons maple syrup or honey

mint leaves, to serve

STRAWBERRY YOGHURT PIZZA BASE

80 g strawberry yoghurt

250 g (1⅔ cups) self-raising flour, plus extra for dusting

THIS IS HOW WE DO IT

To make the strawberry yoghurt pizza base, I like to use a stand mixer with the dough hook attached. Drop the yoghurt and flour into the bowl and mix until you have a ball of dough. Lightly flour your work surface and knead the dough for about 1 minute or until it is smooth. If the dough is a little sticky, simply add a touch more flour and knead again. Place the dough in a lightly oiled bowl, cover with plastic wrap and set aside at room temperature for 20 minutes.

You can make multiple smaller pizzas or one big pizza, as long as it fits in your air fryer. Once you've made this difficult decision, start rolling the dough out until it is 1 cm thick. Line your air fryer with baking paper, then add the pizza base/s and cook on 175°C for 8 minutes (you'll need to cook the bases in batches if you're making smaller pizzas).

Let the pizza base/s cool for 5–10 minutes, then spread the strawberry yoghurt over the top. Add the berries any way you like (get creative), then drizzle over the maple syrup or honey. Scatter over a few mint leaves to replicate basil and you have created a masterpiece. Well done!

MORE THINGS

Don't limit yourself to berries; go tropical with mango, passionfruit and pineapple (this is the only time I'll allow pineapple on a pizza).

You can also turn this into a full-on chocolate pizza by topping it with chocolate–hazelnut spread instead of strawberry yoghurt, then sprinkling over choc chips and drizzling with melted chocolate.

LUNCHBOX INSPO

Kiffli (see page 42) are a bit like Macedonian croissants – yum!

When it comes to kids' lunchboxes, think small! These mini croissants (see page 124) are guaranteed to please.

Mash an avocado and stir through some pitted olives, then sandwich it between pita bread triangles. Easy, colourful and nutritious!

Make mini versions of my pizza to die for (see page 92).

Try making my pizza scrolls (see page 28) with honey and cinnamon instead of cheese and tomato for a delicious sweet treat.

The 'sand-ling' (aka dumpling sandwich). Cut out a round of wholemeal bread using a mug, then flatten with your hand. Fill with grated cheese and ham, then fold and pinch the edges to seal. Boom!

Gevrek (see page 127) make a fun lunchbox addition.

Add some grated cheddar to pieces of pita bread and pop them in the air fryer to melt the cheese – quick and easy!

Use a julienne peeler to create carrot 'noodles' for fussy eaters!

Pop my meatballs (see page 98) in a baguette for a banging sandwich.

You can't go wrong with my air-fried pizza scrolls (see page 28).

The 'rav-wich' (aka ravioli sandwich). Cut the crusts off two slices of wholemeal bread and use a rolling pin to flatten. Place some grated cheese and ham in the four corners of one slice, then top with the other slice and use a ravioli cutter to cut into four squares.

Include your kids' favourite dip for dunking their kiffli (see page 42) into.

My bread rolls (see page 36) are great either plain or filled.

Make wraps more fun by cutting them in half and threading onto wooden skewers with a few cherry tomatoes.

Jazz up cobs of corn with butter, salt and a little smoked paprika.

A generous dollop of mayo makes everything delicious!

Create a rainbow of fruit and veg in your child's lunchbox!

Wrap mushrooms and broccoli florets with bacon, secure with a toothpick and pop them in the air fryer on 180˚C for 5 minutes or until golden. You're welcome.

Try including seed crackers for something a little different.

Your kids will be the envy of the class with my crazy noodle veggies (see page 80).

Use any
cheese you like
to make these
filo pastries (see
page 45).

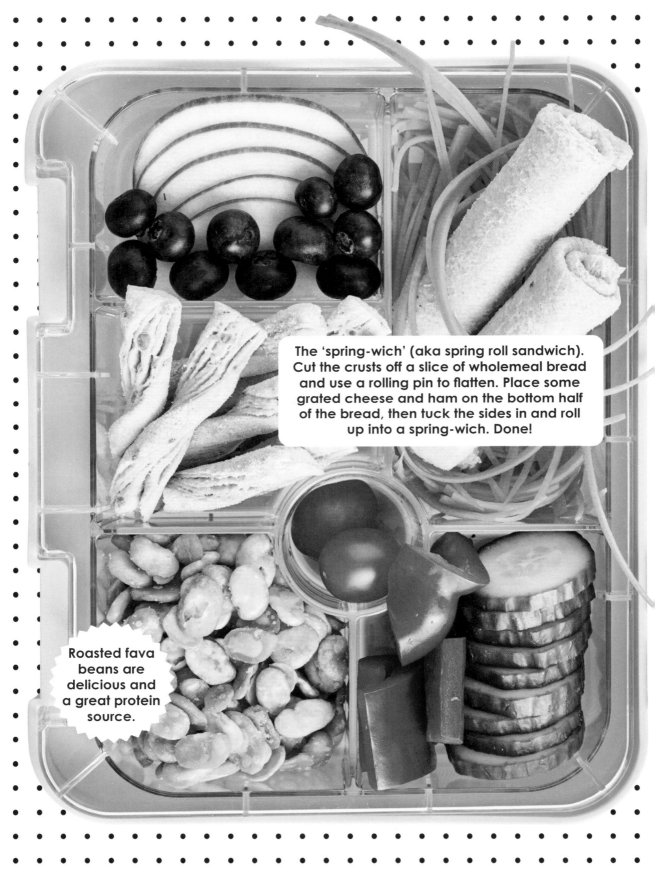

The 'spring-wich' (aka spring roll sandwich). Cut the crusts off a slice of wholemeal bread and use a rolling pin to flatten. Place some grated cheese and ham on the bottom half of the bread, then tuck the sides in and roll up into a spring-wich. Done!

Roasted fava beans are delicious and a great protein source.

Stuff mini capsicums with cream cheese for a hit of veg and dairy.

Make mini versions of my burger patties (see page 86), then add them to burger buns with some cheddar slices.

Store-bought cheese twists are perfect for the lunchbox. Or, if you have the time, my homemade grissini (see page 35) are also great.

Pizza scrolls (see page 28) never get old!

CONVERSION CHARTS

Measuring cups and spoons may vary slightly from one country to another, but the difference is generally not enough to affect a recipe. All cup and spoon measures are level.

One Australian metric measuring cup holds 250 ml (8 fl oz), one Australian tablespoon holds 20 ml (4 teaspoons) and one Australian metric teaspoon holds 5 ml. North America, New Zealand and the UK use a 15 ml (3-teaspoon) tablespoon.

LENGTH

METRIC	IMPERIAL
3 mm	⅛ inch
6 mm	¼ inch
1 cm	½ inch
2.5 cm	1 inch
5 cm	2 inches
18 cm	7 inches
20 cm	8 inches
23 cm	9 inches
25 cm	10 inches
30 cm	12 inches

LIQUID MEASURES

ONE AMERICAN PINT		ONE IMPERIAL PINT
500 ml (16 fl oz)		600 ml (20 fl oz)

CUP	METRIC	IMPERIAL
⅛ cup	30 ml	1 fl oz
¼ cup	60 ml	2 fl oz
⅓ cup	80 ml	2½ fl oz
½ cup	125 ml	4 fl oz
⅔ cup	160 ml	5 fl oz
¾ cup	180 ml	6 fl oz
1 cup	250 ml	8 fl oz
2 cups	500 ml	16 fl oz
2¼ cups	560 ml	20 fl oz
4 cups	1 litre	32 fl oz

DRY MEASURES

The most accurate way to measure dry ingredients is to weigh them. However, if using a cup, add the ingredient loosely to the cup and level with a knife; don't compact the ingredient unless the recipe requests 'firmly packed'.

METRIC	IMPERIAL
15 g	½ oz
30 g	1 oz
60 g	2 oz
125 g	4 oz (¼ lb)
185 g	6 oz
250 g	8 oz (½ lb)
375 g	12 oz (¾ lb)
500 g	16 oz (1 lb)
1 kg	32 oz (2 lb)

OVEN TEMPERATURES

CELSIUS	FAHRENHEIT	CELSIUS	GAS MARK
100°C	200°F	110°C	¼
120°C	250°F	130°C	½
150°C	300°F	140°C	1
160°C	325°F	150°C	2
180°C	350°F	170°C	3
200°C	400°F	180°C	4
220°C	425°F	190°C	5
		200°C	6
		220°C	7
		230°C	8
		240°C	9
		250°C	10

THANK YOU

Mum, you are my rock and inspiration. I love you more than you'll ever know and I feel that this book is as big a part of you as it is of me. These recipes were inspired by you and the amazing childhood you gave me. I love you.

Anela, my first born. I felt the true meaning of love the day you were born.

Kiki, daddy's little girl. When you were little and I used to put you in bed each night, I'd lay beside your bed even when you'd tell me to go to my own room. I'd refuse as I didn't want you to grow up. You've completed my heart.

Marine, you support me in so many ways and you've always fuelled my passion. You've aced solo parenting while I've been travelling and promoting my passion. You just get sh*t done. There is fairy tale love and then there's real, true love. You are my true love. Thank you for everything. Also, having a Ms Universe as a partner is pretty damn special!

Suzy, my big sister and protector. Your enthusiasm for this book and all your help was amazing. There was no way known that I wasn't going to name the pavlova after you – you are the pavlova queen! I love how no one can drink more than you and me. I love you, big sis, and I love how much Anela reminds me of you. I get to relive our childhood again through my relationship with her.

Vince, you're my bro-in-law but you're closer to me than any brother could be. I love you mainly for how much you love my sister, even after 25 years of marriage. Thank you for always taking out the best whisky when I visit. You mean a lot to me, big bro.

Lachlan T, I'm so proud of the respectful, kind and giving human you've become. Now, can I have your runners that you've outgrown please? Those Yeezy ones would do just fine. Love you Lochs.

Jules, my not so little nephew, you are so much like me when I was your age except I wasn't as handsome. Stay as you are and never change, except change your undies daily. Love you Itch.

Warren Freeman, you are my best friend and partner in crime. I can't thank you enough for being my soul mate. We've never had a dull moment and we've created so many amazing memories. But as a human, bro, you have inspired me so much to be a better person and to drink wine from 1967.

Gayle Oznobyshyn-Hicks, you were the one who said I should have a book out and I laughed. Now I've written my second book because of your nudge … okay, it was more of a push. Thank you for helping me make it happen.

Mary Small, the best publisher on the planet. If there were publishers on other planets you'd be the best publisher in the universe. Thank you for taking your chance on this Geelong dad. You clearly have an eye for talent and handsomeness. I know I'm one of many, but you're my one and only. You know I'm going to say it … is this really happening again?

Jane Winning, you are a workaholic (in the best way) and manage to drive me and get the best out of me. I am truly grateful for you taking me under your wing and making it happen. You are a talent and a natural, which has made my job so much easier and more enjoyable. Thank you so much.

Ashley Ellis, you rock! You have a warmth about you that gives me good vibes. You always know how to write down what I feel and that makes you a legend. I'm so grateful I was able to work with you on all my books to date, even though this is only number two. I'm grateful to have had you on my team. You are a legend.

Nikole Ramsay, you brought my food to life with your beautiful photos. I'm in awe of your creativity and ability to get just the right angle. You laughed at my jokes during production and I love you.

Jamie Humby, I knew from our first video chat that we were going to get along like a house on fire and work really well together. You made my food look extra delicious with your crazy styling skills and for that, I'm so grateful. You're a real calming dude and you make me burst with fruit flavour with your creativity.

Jonte Carlson, you're my secret weapon, mate. Your chef skills are amazing and your nursing skills are up there too. I'd gladly cut my finger again knowing you're there to fix me up. You're a genuine great guy, full of awesomeness. Thank you for working by my side to create my dream.

Kirby Armstrong, thank you for your incredible design work once again. You absolutely brought my words and recipes to life and captured my personality in this bright and fun little package.

Lucy Heaver, thank you for your excellent editing work making sure my recipes are perfect while also keeping in most of my dad jokes.

Karina Duncan and The KO, thank you for the truly beautiful shoot location and for allowing us to use your props. It's awesome to have such an incredible space so close to where I live in G-town.

Eddie Vedder from Pearl Jam, you actually played a big role in my young adulthood and although we haven't met (yet!), your music and lyrics saved my life. Peace out EV.

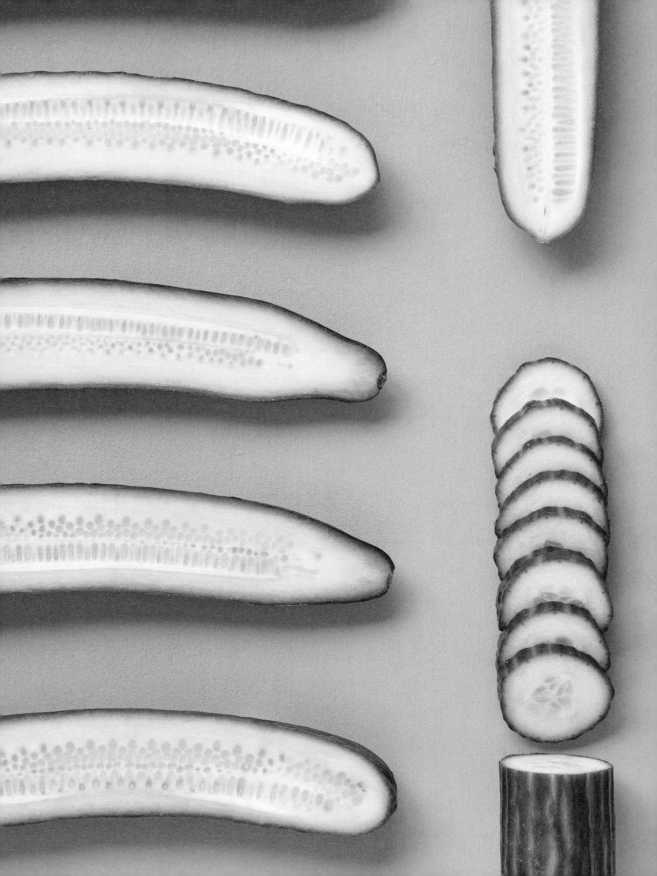

INDEX

A Plum book

First published in 2021 by
Pan Macmillan Australia Pty Limited
Level 25, 1 Market Street,
Sydney, NSW 2000, Australia

Level 3, 112 Wellington Parade,
East Melbourne, VIC 3002, Australia

Design and typesetting by Kirby Armstrong
Edited by Lucy Heaver
Index by Helena Holmgren
Photography by Nikole Ramsay
Prop and food styling by Jamie Humby
Food preparation by George Georgievski and Jonte Carlson
Colour reproduction by Splitting Image Colour Studio
Printed and bound in China by 1010 Printing International Limited

A CIP catalogue record for this book is available from the National Library
of Australia.

The publisher would like to thank Karina Duncan and Stuck On You for their
generosity in providing props for the book.

10 9 8 7 6 5 4 3 2